10/02

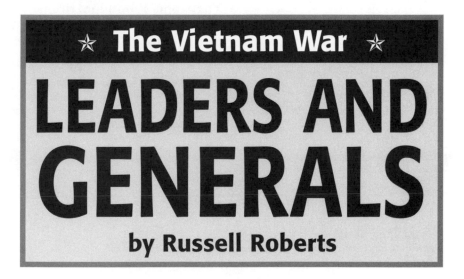

The Vietnam War

LEADERS AND GENERALS

by Russell Roberts

Lucent Books, P.O. Box 289011, San Diego, CA 92198-9011

Titles in The American War Library series include:

World War II
Hitler and the Nazis
Kamikazes
Leaders and Generals
Life as a POW
Life of an American Soldier in
 Europe
Strategic Battles in Europe
Strategic Battles in the Pacific
The War at Home
Weapons of War

The Civil War
Leaders of the North and South
Life Among the Soldiers and
 Cavalry
Lincoln and the Abolition of
 Slavery

Strategic Battles
Weapons of War

The Persian Gulf War
Leaders and Generals
Life of an American Soldier
The War Against Iraq
Weapons of War

The Vietnam War
A History of U.S. Involvement
The Home Front: Americans
 Protest the War
Leaders and Generals
Life of an American Soldier
Life as a POW
Weapons of War

Library of Congress Cataloging-in-Publication Data

Roberts, Russell, 1953–
    Leaders and generals / by Russell Roberts.
        p. cm. — (American war library. Vietnam War)
    Includes bibliographical references and index.
        ISBN 1-56006-717-9 (lib. bdg. : alk. paper)
Summary: Discusses the leaders and generals of the Vietnam War, in-
cluding: Ho Chi Minh, Ngo Dinh Diem, Lyndon B. Johnson, William
Westmoreland, Richard Nixon, and Henry Kissinger.

⋆ **Contents** ⋆

A Nation Forged by War

he United States, like many nations, was forged and defined by war. Despite Benjamin Franklin's opinion that "There never was a good war or a bad peace," the United States owes its very existence to the War of Independence, one to which Franklin wholeheartedly subscribed. The country forged by war in 1776 was tempered and made stronger by the Civil War in the 1860s.

The Texas Revolution, the Mexican-American War, and the Spanish-American War expanded the country's borders and gave it overseas possessions. These wars made the United States a world power, but this status came with a price, as the nation became a key but reluctant player in both World War I and World War II.

Each successive war further defined the country's role on the world stage. Following World War II, U.S. foreign policy redefined itself to focus on the role of defender, not only of the freedom of its own citizens, but also of the freedom of people everywhere. During the cold war that followed World War II until the collapse of the Soviet Union, defending the world meant fighting communism. This goal, manifested in the Korean and Vietnam conflicts, proved elusive, and soured the American public on its achievability. As the United States emerged as the world's sole superpower, American foreign policy has been guided less by national interest and more on protecting international human rights. But as involvement in Somalia and Kosovo prove, this goal has been equally elusive.

As a result, the country's view of itself changed. Bolstered by victories in World Wars I and II, Americans first relished the role of protector. But, as war followed war in a seemingly endless procession, Americans began to doubt their leaders, their motives, and themselves. The Vietnam War especially caused people to question the validity of sending its young people to die in places where they were not particularly wanted and for people who did not seem especially grateful.

While the most obvious changes brought about by America's wars have been geopolitical in nature, many other aspects of society have been touched. War often does not bring about change directly, but acts instead like the catalyst in a chemical reaction, accelerating changes already in progress.

Some of these changes have been societal. The role of women in the United States had been slowly changing, but World War II put thousands into the workforce and into uniform. They might have gone back to being housewives after the war, but equality, once experienced, would not be forgotten.

Likewise, wars have accelerated technological change. The necessity for faster airplanes and a more destructive bomb led to the development of jet planes and nuclear energy. Artificial fibers developed for parachutes in the 1940s were used in the clothing of the 1950s.

Lucent Books' American War Library covers key wars in the development of the nation. Each war is covered in several volumes, to allow for more detail, context, and to provide volumes on often neglected subjects, such as the kamikazes of World War II, or weapons used in the Civil War. As with all Lucent Books, notes, annotated bibliographies, and appendixes such as glossaries give students a launching point for further research. In addition, sidebars and archival photographs enhance the text. Together, each volume in The American War Library will aid students in understanding how America's wars have shaped and changed its politics, economics, and society.

A Protracted Struggle

Although the first U.S. combat troops did not splash ashore in South Vietnam until early 1965, in reality foreign involvement in Vietnam dates back much further.

For decades, beginning in the later half of the nineteenth century, France ruled Vietnam as part of its Southeast Asian colonial empire. Although the Japanese conquest of the region during World War II expelled the French from the territory, they returned to Vietnam after the war ended in 1945, determined to reestablish their dominance over the area. The following year war broke out between France and the Viet Minh, a Communist group led by Ho Chi Minh that was trying to obtain Vietnam's independence.

For eight years the war raged. Although France's armed forces were technically superior, the Viet Minh had the advantage of support from Vietnam's vast peasant population. Finally, after suffering a devastating defeat in the Battle of Dien Bien Phu in May 1954, the French realized that they could never win the war and began seeking a negotiated peace.

The Geneva Accords ending the war between France and the Viet Minh were signed on July 20, 1954. The agreement called for Vietnam to be temporarily split into two nations along the seventeenth parallel. A demilitarized zone (DMZ) was established for five kilometers on either side of the line to prevent armed clashes, and national elections were set for July 1956 to reunify the country. The Communist Viet Minh ruled the north while a non-Communist government took power in the south.

With France eliminated as a force in Vietnamese affairs, the United States was afraid that the Communists would take over all of Vietnam, since Communist leader Ho Chi Minh was such a popular figure to the Vietnamese people. This belief was consistent with what was known as the Domino Theory. According to the Domino

Theory, if one country in a region turned Communist, it would start a chain of events that would culminate in all of the countries becoming Communist, much as a row of dominoes will topple in succession if the first one is knocked over.

Although France was one of the first nations to employ the Domino Theory as its reason for fighting a Communist regime, the theory gained credibility in America when President Dwight Eisenhower used it to explain U.S. involvement

President Eisenhower used the Domino Theory to justify U.S. aid to South Vietnam.

Diem in southern Vietnam so that it could resist the Communist north.

From this simple beginning, America's involvement in Vietnam slowly and steadily expanded throughout the 1950s and early 1960s. However, it seemed that no matter how much aid the United States supplied in the form of arms and advisers, South Vietnam never had enough to put their armed forces on an even keel with the Communists. Eventually American combat troops were called in to try to turn the tide, and soon the United States found itself embroiled in a major war in Southeast Asia.

Before it was over, the Vietnam War destroyed the reputation of one American president, damaged the U.S. economy, fractured both American and Vietnamese society, and wreaked unparalleled devastation on the country of Vietnam. The story of that war is in many ways the story of the men who helped lead their respective nations' war efforts.

in Southeast Asia. Operating under this concept, the U.S. government began supplying aid to the government of Ngo Dinh

Chapter 1

Ho Chi Minh

Ho Chi Minh represented different things to different people. For the United States during the Vietnam War, Ho Chi Minh personified the enemy. For years his thin face with its unruly goatee was the personification of North Vietnam to Americans. For some Vietnamese, Ho Chi Minh was a brutal tyrant who sought to enslave them under the banner of Communism, while for others, Ho Chi Minh was a liberator who sought to throw off the yoke of colonialism and gain independence.

Enemy, tyrant, liberator—this was the paradox of Ho Chi Minh. He was all those things, and yet he was none of them. What he was, above all else, was a nationalist who fought relentlessly for Vietnamese independence and freedom from domination by a foreign power, be it European, Asian, or American. To achieve that goal, he adopted many identities, but he never obscured his one true role: Vietnamese patriot.

A Life of Mystery

The man who would someday be known throughout the world as Ho Chi Minh was born Nguyen Sinh Cung in 1890 in a village in central Vietnam's Nghe Thinh province. Because Ho never kept diaries, wrote memoirs, or dictated his experiences to a biographer, the story of his life is riddled with mystery and confusion. For instance, some historians say that his father abandoned the family, while others claim that his mother died when he was ten and that his father brought him up.

What is certain is that Ho's father, Nguyen Sinh Sac, was a peasant's son who defied traditions to attend school and become a learned man. Juggling both menial farmwork and his studies, he passed an exam in Chinese literature and earned the title of *pho bang* (a minor doctoral degree).

Because of his education, Sac seemed headed for a job in the French colonial administration that governed Vietnam in the early 1900s. But Sac was an ardent nation-

For many years, Ho Chi Minh's face was the personification of North Vietnam to many Americans.

French had caused him to lose his government job.

For the remainder of his life, Sac wandered throughout Indochina as a combination doctor and philosopher. He set broken bones, prepared native medicines, wrote letters for the illiterate, and helped keep his nation's history alive by telling stories of Vietnam's past.

Already exposed to his father's fierce nationalism, Ho (who, at age ten, took a new name—Nguyen Tat Thanh—according to Vietnamese custom) was also greatly influenced by his great-uncle, who espoused Vietnamese independence as well. Together, these two fervent nationalists undoubtedly contributed to Ho's own ardor for Vietnamese freedom.

Although he enrolled in several schools, Ho's nationalistic feelings caused him to constantly clash with his teachers, who tried to promote French culture and foster loyalty to France in their students. Finally while still a teenager he left school without a diploma and traveled to southern Vietnam, where he briefly taught school in the fishing village of Phan Thiet before settling in the city of Saigon.

Seeker of Knowledge

Convinced that he must learn more about the Westerners who dominated his country, Ho set out to explore their lands, in the hope that this knowledge held the key to

alist who yearned for Vietnam's independence and who disliked the French. Although he worked at the imperial court in Hue, Sac refused to learn French because he felt it would taint his own language. Although chroniclers disagree on exactly when, by 1915 Sac's obvious distaste for the freeing Vietnam from foreign rule. In 1911 he signed up under the name Van Ba to serve as a mess boy on the French freighter *Admiral Latouche Treville*. When the ship steamed out of Saigon harbor, it was the last time Ho would see Vietnam for three decades.

Ho's global travels were instructive. On a trip to France's colonies in Africa, he saw that the French treated the Africans as badly as they did the Vietnamese. "In France," said Ho, "the French are very good; but in the colonies these Frenchmen are very mean, very inhuman. . . . For these colonials, the life of yellow or black people doesn't count at all."[1]

After stops in Boston and San Francisco and a year-long stay in New York, Ho settled in London, where he found work as an assistant to the famous pastry chef Georges-Auguste Escoffier at the elegant Carlton Hotel.

Paris

Although Ho was an excellent pastry chef, the cause of Vietnamese independence was his overriding concern in life. Thus in 1917 he moved on again, this time to Paris; the city was home to a Vietnamese population of more than one hundred thousand, whom Ho felt were ripe for conversion to the cause of independence. Adopting the name Nguyen Ai Quoc (Nguyen the Patriot), Ho plunged into the political maelstrom that was Paris at that time.

The budding revolutionary couldn't have found a better place to feed his na-

In Paris, Ho found the perfect environment in which to foster his revolutionary ideas.

tionalist appetite. World War I, plus the overthrow of the czar and rise to power of the Bolsheviks in Russia, seemed to herald a new world order and an end to colonialism. Paris seethed with talk of revolt. Ho immersed himself in this world: He surrounded himself with anarchists and wrote left-wing tracts for political magazines. He even wrote a political play, titled *The Bamboo Dragon*, about a corrupt Asian king who was supposedly modeled after the current emperor of Vietnam, Khai Dinh. The play was not a success, however, and closed after one performance.

As part of his political activity, Ho read voraciously. One of the most influential books for him was *Das Kapital* by Karl Marx, a work destined to become a cornerstone of modern communism. Ho felt

Among the many books that Ho read was Das Kapital *by Karl Marx (pictured).*

that Marx's appeal to the workers of the world to rise up against the ruling classes could be used to incite the Vietnamese population to reject their foreign masters. Under Marx's influence, Ho developed a political philosophy that combined fierce nationalism with communism.

Disappointment at Versailles

The end of World War I on November 11, 1918, offered Ho the chance to put his philosophy to the test. Early in 1919, the victorious Allied nations met at the palace of Versailles outside Paris to negotiate the peace treaty that would formally end the war. Among the issues to be discussed was what was to be done with the colonies held by the nations involved in the fighting.

Ho felt that this conference represented a new start for oppressed nations all over the world. He wrote: "All subject peoples are filled with hope by the prospect that an era of right and justice is opening to them . . . in the struggle of civilization against barbarism."[2] Fired by his passion, Ho went to Versailles, where he hoped to present his own eight-point program for Vietnamese independence to the victorious Allies.

But it was not to be. The freedom that the Allied leaders discussed at Versailles was freedom for European nations, not for their Asian and African colonies. Ho was unable to present his eight-point program, or meet U.S. President Woodrow Wilson, whose call to freely and impartially settle colonial claims as part of his plan for a peace treaty had filled Ho with hope.

But although he had failed in Versailles, Ho succeeded in raising his stature within France's Vietnamese community simply because he had made the effort. As a Vietnamese student said: "No two Vietnamese residing in France could meet after this without mentioning the name of Nguyen Ai Quoc."[3]

Thanks to his new celebrity, Ho was invited to address an important meeting of the French Socialist political party held in the town of Tours. Here, surrounded by influential Socialists, Ho asked for help in freeing Vietnam from French rule. "In the name of all mankind, in the name of all socialists, right wing or left wing, we appeal to you, comrades. Save us!"[4] he begged.

A New Philosophy

But like his failed trip to Versailles, the conference was a disappointment for Ho. The Socialists seemed content to debate theories and opinions about revolution and wait for peaceful, parliamentary change. This measured approach was too slow and uncertain a path for Ho. The Communists, on the other hand, after their victory in Russia, seemed ready to spread their revolution wherever they could and help foster it using every method at their disposal, including violence, if necessary. Feeling that communism would be more beneficial to the Vietnamese cause, Ho helped found

the French Communist Party on December 30, 1920.

In addition to these efforts on behalf of Vietnam, Ho gathered all of the pro-independence groups in the French empire into an organization called the Intercolonial Union. Because of his role in forming these two groups, and also because he wrote for several pro-Communist newspapers, the French police placed Ho under surveillance.

Ho knew that, despite his direct experience, he still had much to learn if he was going to succeed in freeing Vietnam. To further his education as a revolutionary, in 1923 Ho went to Moscow. He attended the University of Oriental Workers, where he learned revolutionary strategies and tactics. He also wrote articles for Soviet publications, although a representative from Germany recalled Ho at this time as being "far more inclined towards action than towards doctrinal debates."[5]

Apparently Ho learned his revolutionary lessons well, for late in 1924 his Communist superiors sent him to Canton, China. He was assigned to help the Russian advisor to the new revolutionary Chinese government, one of whose leaders was Chiang Kai-shek. Under the pseudonym of Ly Thuy, Ho worked on a variety of projects in China, including the founding of the Revolutionary Youth League, an organization of young exiled Vietnamese. Ho taught his new recruits Marxist theory as well as practical advice, including how to avoid detection by the authorities by organizing in small groups. He also showed them how to attract converts to communism by addressing specific social problems rather than spouting revolutionary rhetoric. "Peasants," Ho said, "believe in facts, not theories."[6]

Ho's stay in China ended abruptly in 1927, when Chiang Kai-shek suddenly turned on his Communist allies, killing many in a surprise purge. Ho fled back to Moscow. With time on his hands he toured European castles and cathedrals. Slipping into Paris, he grew nostalgic for the city and wistful about the direction of his life. He said to a friend:

I always thought I would become a scholar or a writer, but I've become a professional revolutionary. I travel through many countries, but I see nothing. I'm on strict orders, and my itinerary is carefully prescribed, and you cannot deviate from the route, can you?[7]

Life of a Revolutionary

Eventually Ho's days of leisure ended, and his superiors in Moscow sent him on another series of globe-trotting missions. He spent time in Buddhist temples in Thailand,

A Chinese peasant stops near some fields. Ho astutely observed that peasants "believe in facts, not theories."

where he shaved his head, pretending to be a Buddhist priest while spreading Communist doctrine. Next he went to Hong Kong, where he fused three different exiled Vietnamese Communist groups trying to oust the French into an umbrella organization called the Indochinese Communist Party (ICP).

As part of these activities, Ho journeyed back and forth between China and the Soviet Union throughout the 1930s. His modes of travel were never luxurious; often they were cramped quarters on freighters or else tiny train compartments. Sometimes the travel was dangerous, such as when he undertook a perilous five-day trip over narrow, rocky trails across the mountains of central China to reach the headquarters of the Chinese Communist Party. His diet often consisted of food that was either bad or simply inedible, and his body frequently had to adjust to temperatures that varied from frigid in one country to torrid in another a week later.

As a result of the inhospitable conditions under which he worked, Ho's health suffered. He contracted tuberculosis and also suffered from amoebic dysentery and recurrent bouts of malaria. But despite these illnesses, Ho remained dedicated to his cause. A friend at the time described Ho as "taut and quivering, with only one thought in his head, his country, Vietnam."[8]

Because he was a known revolutionary, wherever he went the authorities constantly monitored Ho's actions. In June 1931, he was arrested in Hong Kong because of his activities with the ICP. Released with the help of British lawyer Frank Loseby, Ho was diagnosed as tubercular and ordered sent to England for treatment. However the Hong Kong police would not give up and charged him with illegal departure. When Ho's ship stopped in Singapore before leaving for Great Britain, Ho was removed from it and taken back to Hong Kong, where he was placed in a prison infirmary. Loseby again managed to free Ho, and this time got him safely to China.

Before he left for China, however, Ho convinced an infirmary employee to report him as dead—perhaps to take the heat off his activities. His obituary was printed in the Soviet press, and the French closed his file with a notation that he had died in jail in Hong Kong. In Moscow, despondent Vietnamese students held a memorial service for him.

A New Oppressor

But Ho was very much alive, and in 1938 he returned to China to teach guerrilla warfare to Communist forces that were once again allied with Chiang Kai-shek to fight the Japanese Army, which had invaded China in 1937. The invasion of China was only the beginning of Japan's aggressions as part of the wider conflagration that ultimately became World War II. As the war progressed Japanese forces swept through Southeast Asia, wresting control of Vietnam from France, Malaysia from Great

Japanese forces quickly swept through Southeast Asia in the early days of World War II.

felt differently. He saw Japan as just another oppressor, noting that to align with the Japanese would be to "drive the tiger out the front door while letting the wolf in through the back."[9]

For this reason Ho supported the Allies in their effort to defeat Germany and Japan in World War II. He reasoned that the war would leave all the major powers so exhausted that they wouldn't be concerned about reclaiming their former colonies. Ho foresaw that a power vacuum would exist in places like Vietnam—a vacuum that could be filled by a well-organized indigenous group prepared to govern the country.

Operating under this theory, Ho slipped into Vietnam early in 1941, the first time in thirty years that he had been back to his native country. In a mountainous region near the Chinese border, Ho formed a new political party: the Vietnam Doc Lap Dong Minh (the League for Vietnamese Independence), or Viet Minh for short.

In June 1941, Ho listed the goals of the Viet Minh in a radio broadcast that was heard throughout Vietnam. Calling on the Vietnamese to rise up and fight for their freedom, Ho said: "Let us unite together! As one in mind and strength we shall overthrow the Japanese and French and their

Britain, Indonesia from the Netherlands, and the Philippines from the United States.

Although many Asian nationalists greeted the Japanese as liberators who had finally banished the colonial powers, Ho

17

jackals in order to save people from the situation between boiling water and burning heat."[10]

It was also around this time that he changed his name for the final time. Seeking something that would be more nationalistic than his past names, which were associated more with his Communist activities, he chose Ho Chi Minh—roughly translated as "He Who Enlightens."

Although the Japanese controlled Vietnam, they had chosen to keep the French colonial administration in place and give orders from behind the scenes. As the world war raged, Ho and his assistant Vo Nguyen Giap shaped the Viet Minh into a fighting force, helped in large part by small arms and other equipment supplied by the United States.

By the beginning of 1945, the Allies had gained the upper hand in the war, and both Germany and Japan were reeling from repeated defeats. On March 9, 1945, the Japanese, reacting to rumors of an upcoming attack by French troops to regain control of Indochina, suddenly and brutally attacked the French colonial forces in Vietnam to prevent them from assisting in the operation.

With the French colonial government eliminated, the Japanese granted Vietnam inde-

pendence—but it was independence in name only, because Japan did not relinquish control of the country. Bao Dai, who had been the puppet ruler of Vietnam under the French, agreed to fill the same role under the Japanese.

Ho watched these developments with great interest. Even though Japan was still

A poster of Bao Dai adorns a Saigon hotel. Bao served as puppet ruler of Vietnam under both the French and Japanese.

ruling Vietnam, he knew that with their forces in retreat elsewhere, it was only a matter of time before they would also be forced to leave Vietnam. With both Japan and France gone, the power vacuum that he had foreseen would open. In preparation, he and Giap began moving Viet Minh troops deeper into the country from their bases near the Chinese border. By June 1945, the Viet Minh controlled six provinces in northern Vietnam.

Short-Lived Independence

On August 14, 1945, the opportunity that Ho had been waiting for arrived when Japan surrendered to the Allies. Two days later, Ho exhorted his compatriots to rise up and claim their long-sought freedom: "The oppressed the world over are wresting back their independence. We should not lag behind. Forward! Forward! Under the Viet Minh banner, let us valiantly march forward!"[11] That same day, Viet Minh troops occupied the northern Vietnamese city of Hanoi.

With his Japanese protectors defeated, Bao Dai had no choice but to abdicate, which he did late in August 1945. On September 2, Ho declared the formation of the Democratic Republic of Vietnam, with Hanoi as its capital and himself as its president.

Ironically, despite his fame and the fact that he had striven for Vietnamese independence for decades, the name Ho Chi Minh was virtually unknown to most Vietnamese. Some thought that he might be the famous revolutionary Nguyen Ai Quoc, but for reasons that are unclear, Ho officially denied this.

Ho told his people:

We have wrested our independence from the Japanese and not the French. The French have fled, the Japanese have capitulated, Emperor Bao Dai has abdicated, our people have broken down the fetters which for over a century have tied us down.[12]

In his speech Ho also used phrases that were unknown to his listeners at the time, but which had gained fame in other parts of the world: "We hold the truth that all men are created equal, that they are endowed by their Creator with certain unalienable rights, among them life, liberty, and the pursuit of happiness."[13]

Ho had deliberately borrowed those powerful words from the American Declaration of Independence because he was hopeful that the world powers, particularly the United States, would recognize his government and thus legitimize Vietnam's independence. But once again Ho was destined to be disappointed; the struggle for Vietnamese independence was far from over.

Desperate to still be counted among the great nations of the world in spite of their nation's devastation at the hands of Germany in World War II, the French decided to reestablish their colonial empire. In October 1945, French troops returned to Vietnam and seized control of the southern part of the country.

In the north, Ho and the Viet Minh enjoyed wide popular appeal. However, when the United States decided to support France, and even Ho's old ally the Soviet Union elected not to recognize his government, his hopes of gaining support from other nations were dashed. Knowing that France could use its superior military capability to simply crush his government, Ho decided to negotiate with the French rather than fight them.

Ho had a second reason for avoiding a fight with the French. He believed that neighboring China might take advantage of the confusion caused by a war between France and the Viet Minh to take over Vietnam for itself. While he was confident that France would eventually have to give up control of Vietnam because colonialism was dying in other parts of the world, he had no such illusions about China. Because of its proximity, China would be capable of dominating Vietnam for generations. "It is better to sniff the French dung for a while than to eat China's all our lives,"[14] he said.

For months negotiations between Ho and the French dragged on. Early in March 1946, France sent a military convoy to northern Vietnam to pressure Ho. On March 6, 1946, with war looming, Ho signed an agreement calling for twenty-five thousand French troops to reenter northern Vietnam for five years. However the agreement also recognized Vietnam as a free state with its own government, parliament, army, and finances. Vietnam would

Part of a military convoy, a French soldier and a tank move into North Vietnam in March 1946.

be part of the French Union, which was the new name for the country's old colonial empire.

"I'm not very pleased," Ho remarked about the agreement. "I wanted more than this."[15]

Little did he suspect at the time that the agreement would never be implemented. Over the next several months the attitude of the French government turned against recognition of Vietnam as a free state. Ho went to Paris for more negotiations, but was met by scorn and cynicism. The French were convinced that if war came, they could easily defeat their former colony. "We only need an ordinary police action of eight days to clear out all of you,"[16] sniffed one French official to Ho and his aides.

As the talks went nowhere and tensions mounted, French and Viet Minh troops began skirmishing with each other in various parts of Vietnam. One of the most volatile areas was the northern port city of Haiphong, in which French and Viet Minh troops controlled different parts of the city. On November 23, 1946, after the Viet Minh ignored an order to evacuate their troops from Haiphong, French forces attacked the city.

The First Indochina War

With negotiations at a standstill, Ho now knew that war was inevitable. On December 19, skirmishes between French troops and the Viet Minh in Hanoi quickly escalated into an all-out battle for control of the city. Ho fled Hanoi just in time to avoid capture by French authorities. The First Indochina War had begun.

The French soon found that they had greatly underestimated their opponents. Ho, in fact, had predicted that the French could be beaten, even though the Viet Minh were poorly armed:

> We will be like the elephant and the tiger. When the elephant is strong and rested and near his base, we will retreat. And if the tiger ever pauses, the elephant will impale him on his mighty tusks. But the tiger will not pause, and the elephant will die of exhaustion and loss of blood.[17]

For the next eight years Ho and the Viet Minh made the French elephant bleed. France controlled the cities, but the Viet Minh enjoyed the support of the vast peasant population that lived in the countryside. Although France won numerous battles, this was a war fought primarily for the support of the populace, and consequently it was a war that France could not win.

Ho spent the war years living in the jungles, fields, and mountains like the rest of the Viet Minh. He ate the same limited food, cut his rations when times were tough, and hid behind trees when French bombers came, just like everybody else in his army did.

As the war dragged on, with no end in sight, the French public grew weary of the conflict. Late in November 1953, France began fortifying Dien Bien, a small village with an airstrip in northwestern Vietnam, to prevent the Viet Minh from gaining control of nearby Laos. Although the French reinforced the garrison until it contained 10,800 soldiers and brought in artillery, they failed to secure the mountains that encircled the village—a critical error. Viet Minh troops occupied these strategic high points instead and were able to concentrate their fire down onto the French. Ultimately, Giap had nearly fifty thousand troops surrounding Dien Bien Phu (as the French garrison was called)—a five-to-one advantage.

On March 13, 1954, Giap's forces began attacking the French garrison, first with human wave assaults and then with a siege that prevented supplies and reinforcements from getting into Dien Bien Phu. Heavily outnumbered and hopelessly surrounded, the French finally surrendered on May 7.

Peace—and Problems

With the disaster at Dien Bien Phu, France was forced to admit defeat. On July 20, the French and Vietnamese signed a peace agreement. According to the terms, Vietnam was to be temporarily divided at the seventeenth parallel; Ho and the Viet Minh would control the northern part of the country, and a non-Communist government the south. Elections were to be held in July 1956, following which Vietnam would be united under a single government.

One of Ho's first problems as head of the Democratic Republic of Vietnam, as the northern part of the country was called, was a serious food shortage. Although it had a larger population than the south (16 million to 14 million), the north produced just 40 percent of Vietnam's rice. With the rice supply from the south now shut off due to the division of the country, famine seemed imminent in the north.

In an awkward attempt to encourage more food production, Ho instituted a system in 1955 for redistributing land from the rich to the poor. Although the north had never had large rice plantations like those in the south, Ho and his aides arbitrarily decided that 2 percent of the north's peasant population were "landlords" who needed to be "reeducated" and whose lands were to be seized and redistributed.

The program was a disaster. Many supposed landlords were simply killed. People informed on each other and made up lies about their neighbors to save themselves from being labeled landlords. Anyone who was suspected of having supported the French was executed, as were people who did not wholeheartedly support the Viet Minh. Approximately six thousand peasant farmers died or were sent to forced labor camps.

Finally in August 1956, with North Vietnam torn by bitterness, suspicion, and violence, Ho publicly admitted that the classification system had been a mistake. However, Ho's admission did not end the violence. After those who had been erro-

French forces are taken prisoner by the Viet Minh after their surrender at Dien Bien Phu.

neously classified as landlords were released from prison, they took revenge on those who had spoken against them, and civil unrest continued.

Ho also had political problems. With U.S. encouragement and backing, Ngo Dinh Diem, leader of South Vietnam, had cancelled the 1956 elections called for in the Geneva agreement because he feared that Ho Chi Minh and the Viet Minh would win and that all of Vietnam would be united under Communist rule. Realizing that he might have to fight to unify Vietnam, Ho began building a political and military organization in the south. In 1959 armed conflict

Ho Chi Minh enjoys a visit with some children. He died before he was able to see his dream of a united, independent Vietnam.

broke out between these Communist troops—known as Viet Cong—and troops of the Diem government.

A New Foe

Ho now saw that another war loomed, although he remained confident that his forces would win. In 1962 he told a journalist: "Now the Diem regime is well armed and helped by many Americans. The Americans are stronger than the French. It might take ten years, but our heroic compatriots in the South will defeat them in the end."[18]

Four years after Ho made that prediction, North Vietnam was facing the awesome might of the American military machine. However, Ho was convinced that muscle alone would not be enough to win the war.

"We know the power of our enemies," he said. "We know that the Americans, if they like, can wipe out this city, [Hanoi], as they can wipe out all the principal towns. . . . But that does not weaken our determination to fight to the very end."[19]

The years of hard work under difficult conditions had damaged Ho's health. Early in 1969, his heart began to fail. Soon he was no longer able to work. On September 2, 1969, Ho Chi Minh died at age seventy-nine—his country still at war and still divided. Six years later, however, South Vietnam fell to forces from North Vietnam, and the country was finally united. In his honor, the former capital of South Vietnam, Saigon, was renamed Ho Chi Minh City.

Chapter 2

Ngo Dinh Diem

In 1961 Ngo Dinh Diem, president of South Vietnam, was at the height of his political power. U.S. vice president Lyndon Johnson praised him as the "Winston Churchill of Southeast Asia"[20] and even compared him to George Washington.

Yet, that power and prestige proved fleeting. Just two years later, encouraged by American officials, a group of South Vietnamese generals led a coup against Diem that resulted in his and his brother's deaths. In death, Diem showed just how expendable a leader can be.

Early Life

Ngo Dinh Diem was born in 1901 to a Catholic family in the village of Phu Cam near the ancient Vietnamese capital of Hue. His ancestors had been among the first in Vietnam to convert to Catholicism in the seventeenth century. Diem was christened Jean-Baptiste in the Catholic cathedral in Hue.

At the time of Diem's birth, Vietnam was under French control. His father, Ngo Dinh Kha, served as counselor to Vietnamese emperor Thanh Thai, whom the French had installed as the country's figurehead ruler.

Early in his life, Diem witnessed the uncertainties of living under the influence of a foreign power. In 1907 Thanh Thai began resisting French control. Claiming that the emperor was insane, Vietnam's French masters removed him from the throne and replaced him with his son, Duy Tan. In protest over Thanh Thai's treatment Ngo Dinh Kha quit his post. To support himself and his family, Kha became a farmer.

Although he lost his governmental salary, somehow Kha found the money to educate his six sons. Diem, his third child, worked in the rice fields on the family farm and attended a nearby French Catholic school. He also attended a private school that his father operated.

Government Official

Initially Diem considered a career in the priesthood, but changed his mind because the personal sacrifices required seemed too difficult. He then set his sights on a government career like his father had had. To that end, he studied at the School of Law and Administration in Hanoi, a French-run institution designed to educate the Vietnamese to serve as officials in the colonial government.

After graduation Diem moved quickly through the bureaucracy, and at age twenty-five became a provincial governor. It was at this time, while riding through the rice fields and mountains of his district, that Diem first encountered Communist propaganda pamphlets distributed by indigenous Communist groups seeking Vietnamese independence from France. To counter the Communists' appeal, Diem published his own pamphlets, cleaned up administrative corruption, and improved the conditions for peasants under his jurisdiction. These actions earned him a reputation for integrity, industry, and anticommunism.

By 1933 yet another titular emperor, Bao Dai, was on the throne, and thanks to his success as a provincial governor, Diem was named minister of the interior. Diem was also appointed to a commission that was supposed to examine prospective administrative reforms in Vietnam. When Diem expressed misgivings about the commission, wondering if it would truly lead to reforms or be just for show, a French official told him to "take the job and don't complain."[21]

Ngo Dinh Diem followed his father's example and chose a career in the colonial government.

Diem took the job, but not the rest of the advice. He complained publicly and repeatedly that the French were not giving the Vietnamese a true voice in their own government. After three contentious months Diem quit Bao Dai's government, proclaiming that he could not "act against the interests of my country."[22] As punishment, the French stripped Diem of his titles and decorations, and threatened to arrest him.

A Hero among His People

Having spoken out against both the Communists and the French, as well as in favor of Vietnamese independence, Diem became a hero among his compatriots. Lacking the fiery spirit of a revolutionary, however, Diem chose not to instigate or participate in armed resistance. Instead, he withdrew to his mother's home in Hue, where he kept in contact with other Vietnamese nationalists both at home and abroad.

For the next twelve years, Diem kept a low profile, but when in August 1945 Communist leader Ho Chi Minh unofficially proclaimed an independent Vietnamese republic with himself as president, Diem felt that he had to act. Diem set out to see former emperor Bao Dai, who had been deposed by Ho, and warn him not to join forces with the Communists.

Diem never made it to see Bao Dai. Communist Viet Minh troops captured him en route and exiled him to a primitive village near the Chinese border. There he contracted malaria and nearly died. While at the village, Diem learned that the Viet Minh had murdered both his brother Khoi and Khoi's son.

Confrontation with the Communists

The Viet Minh confined Diem to the village for several months. Early in 1946, they took him to Hanoi to meet Ho Chi Minh.

Because of his opposition to the Communist regime, Diem was exiled to a primitive village like this one.

France had proven unwilling to concede Vietnamese independence and had landed troops in Vietnam to try and reestablish control over its colony. Ho asked Diem to join with him to fight the French, but Diem refused. He called Ho "a criminal who has burned and destroyed the country."[23] He went on to accuse the Viet Minh of killing his brother. Then Diem challenged Ho, saying that he would always be a free man and would never bow to pressure to work with the Communists. To Diem's surprise, Ho admitted that Diem was indeed free and let him walk out of the room, ending his captivity.

Diem continued to oppose Ho, although he also refused to back the French. Although skirmishes had occurred in November 1946, when full-scale fighting broke out between the Viet Minh and the French in December 1946, Diem issued a declaration calling on France to give Vietnam its independence. Bao Dai, who the French were bringing back as emperor, asked him to become prime minister in his government, but Diem refused. Instead, he formed a nationalist party that opposed both the French and the Viet Minh. Diem's reputation grew among his people as a man who would not compromise his principles and who was devoted to the cause of Vietnamese independence.

Diem's anticommunist reputation, coupled with his popularity with the Vietnamese, made him a threat to the Viet Minh. In the late 1940s, they condemned him to death in absentia, and assassins from the Viet Minh attempted to kill him during a trip he made to visit his brother Thuc.

Exile

Realizing that Vietnam had become too dangerous for him, Diem left his homeland in 1950 and made his way to the United States. For two years he lived at the Maryknoll Seminary in Lakewood, New Jersey. There he washed dishes, scrubbed floors, and waited for an opportunity to serve Vietnam.

While Diem was scrubbing floors, U.S. Supreme Court justice William O. Douglas, disturbed by the U.S. policy of supporting the French only because they opposed Ho Chi Minh and the Communists, was visiting Vietnam to get a firsthand look at the area. Douglas thought that there had to be a better means of establishing a noncommunist government in Vietnam.

While in Vietnam, Douglas was approached by numerous people who claimed that they were nationalists opposed to both French rule and communism. They told him about a man named Diem, who had been forced to leave the country because of his unwillingness to work with either the Communists or the French. Diem, one individual told him, was "revered by the Vietnamese because he is honest and independent and stood firm against French influence—a hero in Central and North Vietnam, with considerable following in the South too."[24]

Convinced that he had found a viable, noncommunist alternative to French rule

Supreme Court justice William O. Douglas (pictured) felt that Diem could provide stable, noncommunist leadership to Vietnam.

in Vietnam, Douglas returned to the United States determined to get the United States to back Diem. In May 1953, Douglas hosted a luncheon in Washington, D.C., to which he invited Diem. Among those in attendance was Senator John F. Kennedy from Massachusetts. Kennedy had also recently toured Vietnam, and like Douglas had become convinced that U.S.

policy toward the country was on the wrong track.

Diem spoke at the luncheon, and his staunch anticommunism and passion for Vietnamese independence made a favorable impression on those in attendance. He told his audience that the French would never defeat the Viet Minh. Only the Vietnamese themselves could do that, Diem asserted, and only after they gained their independence.

Thanks to the impression he made at this luncheon, Diem began gaining supporters in the U.S. government. These individuals saw him as the only leader who could prevent a Communist takeover of Vietnam. As it happened, despite his closeness to the French, Bao Dai also viewed Diem the same way. As the war dragged on with little hope for a French victory, Bao Dai knew that the entire country would fall to the Communists unless a substitute for France's protection could be found. Although Diem had no official backing from the United States, Bao Dai believed that his presence in the Vietnamese government would be enough to pull the United States into the role of Vietnam's protector.

Return to Vietnam

Early in 1954, Bao Dai again asked Diem to become prime minister in his government. This time Diem accepted—none too soon,

Two French soldiers run for cover during the Battle of Dien Bien Phu.

Bao Dai undoubtedly felt, because on May 7 the Viet Minh defeated the French at Dien Bien Phu, causing France to seek ne-

gotiations to end the war. On June 26, 1954, Diem returned to Vietnam.

One month later, in Geneva, Switzerland, the defeated French signed an agreement that ended the war with the Viet Minh. The accord temporarily divided Vietnam into two nations along the seventeenth parallel. The Communist government of Ho

Chi Minh was left in control of the northern portion and the non-Communist government of Diem and Bao Dai controlled the south. According to the agreement, national elections were to be held in July 1956 to reunify Vietnam under a single government.

Although the Geneva treaty ended the war, it satisfied neither the United States nor Diem. With the defeat of France, the United States saw its worst fears realized: There was no organized opposition to Ho Chi Minh and the Communists, who seemed almost certain to win the 1956 election, thanks to the popular support they enjoyed from their long struggle against the French. To prevent that from happening, the United States began assisting Diem's government. U.S. officials, invoking what became known as the Domino Theory, worried that if Vietnam turned Communist, other nations in the region would follow.

For Diem, the loss of half his country to the Communists was a severe blow to his desire of ruling a united Vietnam. Himself a devout Catholic, he had been counting on support from Catholic areas in the north. The division of Vietnam into two countries effectively closed off the north and south from each other, both politically and socially. Accordingly, Diem declared the day the Geneva Accords were signed a "Day of Infamy" and ordered flags flown at half-mast on all official buildings in the south.

Diem also had other problems. The Communist takeover of northern Vietnam caused a mass exodus from that region of Catholics and others that had opposed the Viet Minh. Eventually, 860,000 people fled to the south, placing a huge strain on Diem's government as it tried to provide for the refugees' needs. At the same time, Diem was trying to consolidate his control over his army, which was headed by an officer sympathetic to the French named Nguyen Van Hinh. Hinh's outspoken opposition to Diem gave rise to rumors that he was going to attempt a coup against Diem. Adding to Diem's woes was that he was also battling several armed groups that controlled large parts of southern Vietnam, running them like their own private fiefdoms. In the face of all these problems, Bao Dai fled to France, leaving Diem to sort things out on his own.

President of South Vietnam

But with help Diem overcame the challenges to his rule. Thanks to clear signals from American officials that they opposed a coup attempt, Diem gained control over the army. With the military under his control, he attacked the armed groups in the spring of 1955, smashing their power and influence. Diem then moved to consolidate his hold on the political process by scheduling a referendum in October 1955, giving voters in the south the chance to choose between him and Bao Dai as chief of state.

During this election Diem's autocratic tendencies began to show. Henchmen working for Diem were present at many polling stations, forcing people to vote for him. As one voter recalled:

> They told us to put the red ballot [for Diem] into envelopes and throw the green ones [for Bao Dai] into the wastebasket. A few people, faithful to Bao Dai, disobeyed. As soon as they left, the agents went after them, and roughed them up. The agents poured pepper sauce down their nostrils, or forced water down their throats. They beat one of my relatives to a pulp.[25]

Thanks to tactics like these, the election was not a true test of Diem's support, even though he claimed victory with 98.2 percent of the vote. Irregularities were rampant, such as in Saigon, the capital city of southern Vietnam, in which Diem said he received over 600,000 votes even though only 450,000 voters were registered in the entire city.

Although he was in complete charge of southern Vietnam, Diem and his U.S. backers still knew that to pit him against Ho Chi Minh in an election would likely result in a Communist takeover of all Vietnam. Therefore, Diem again denounced the 1956 elections mandated by the Geneva Accords on the grounds that they could not be "absolutely free."[26] Then on October 26, 1955, Diem proclaimed southern Vietnam to be the Republic of Vietnam (also known as South Vietnam) and himself as the new nation's president. In March of the following year a new 123-member legislative assembly was elected that was totally loyal to Diem. With U.S. support, Diem then refused to hold the reunification elections on grounds that his government had never agreed to them.

Shaky Ground

To outsiders, Diem's apparent success in bringing stability to his nation seemed remarkable. During Diem's visit to the United States in May 1957, President Dwight Eisenhower praised Diem as a "miracle man."[27] Yet the foundation upon which his miracles stood was shaky.

One problem for Diem's regime was that his desire to eliminate elements of the Viet Minh that remained in the south following the signing of the Geneva Accords had turned into a vendetta against anyone who once was even remotely involved with the Communists. Many people who only wanted now to live in peace were either forced into hiding or killed by Diem's troops. These actions turned many peasants against Diem. Driven underground, many Viet Minh veterans became the backbone of the National Liberation Front (commonly called Viet Cong), a Communist insurrectionist group formed in South Vietnam in 1960.

In addition to wreaking vengeance on suspected Communist sympathizers, Diem further angered peasants by allowing wealthy landowners to retain large amounts of land rather than redistributing it to the poor. Diem had hoped that by placating the landowners in this way, he would convince

With his henchmen forcing voters to vote for him, Diem claimed victory in the South Vietnamese elections with 98.2 percent of the vote.

his government had taken control.

As his popularity with the peasants fell and the influence of the Communists rose, Diem took more drastic measures to limit that influence. Large numbers of peasants were relocated to new communities called *agrovilles*, which South Vietnamese troops protected—the plan being that people could live and work without fear of intimidation by the Communists. The relocation program was a failure, however. From the peasants' perspective, Diem was uprooting them from their longtime homes and forcing them to live far away from the land, traditions, and graves of their ancestors.

An Isolated Leader

The success or failure of his policies had little effect on Diem. Relying on his surviving brothers for support and advice, Diem was isolated from the ordinary people of Vietnam. Among his brothers, Diem particularly relied on Nhu, who was head of the national police. Nhu used the organization to gather information on the political activities of people throughout the country. The repressive tactics of Nhu's police further alienated the Vietnamese from their president.

them to become part of his political base. Diem then compounded his error by ordering peasants to pay for land that the Viet Minh had given them earlier, before

Thanks to his isolation, Diem's policies tended to more and more favor a small group of wealthy landowners, businesspeople, relatives, and some military officers, while ignoring the needs of the peasants. Yet even more damaging to him was that he was becoming increasingly alienated from his supporters in the United States.

A Government in Peril

By April 1960, the United States had spent more than a billion dollars on aid to South Vietnam. Yet Diem was becoming more and more antagonistic toward his benefactors. Diem was, as one American official noted, "a puppet who pulled his own strings."[28] He could act this way because he knew he was operating from a position of strength: South Vietnam, Diem knew, was considered a key component of the U.S. foreign policy strategy of containing communism in Southeast Asia. As long as America considered Diem to be a bulwark against the spread of communism to other countries in the region, the United States needed him.

In his isolation, Diem failed to realize that his autocratic, corrupt government was trying the patience of his own people. In April 1960, eighteen well-known Vietnamese nationalists presented a petition to Diem, asking for government reforms. Instead, he closed opposition newspapers and arrested students, journalists

and other intellectuals on the charge of having Communist affiliations.

Diem's unpopularity was further underscored just seven months later when

Diem is shown taking businessmen and advisors on a tour of his summer estate. As time went on, Diem completely isolated himself from the ordinary Vietnamese people.

members of his army attempted to overthrow his government. Diem agreed to free elections and other reform measures that the rebels demanded, but in reality he was just playing for time until military units loyal to him could crush the rebellion. As soon as the coup had been suppressed, Diem reneged on his promises of reform and arrested more supposed Communists.

Relationship Worsens with the United States

This coup attempt was critical to Diem's relationship with the United States. When the outcome was still in doubt, the U.S. ambassador to South Vietnam, Elbridge Durbrow, had urged Diem to negotiate with the rebels, thereby proving to the South Vietnamese president that he did not enjoy unequivocal American support. Moreover, Diem suspected that the United States had actually participated in planning the coup. Soon his influential sister-in-law, the fiery and outspoken Madame Nhu, began making speeches in which she blamed South Vietnam's problems on America.

Although the United States denied involvement in the attempted coup, Diem's increased intransigence and growing coolness toward the United States now triggered thoughts in American government circles of finding a replacement. "We may well be forced, in the not too distant future, to undertake the difficult task of identifying and supporting alternative leadership,"[29] Durbow said to his superiors on December 4, 1960.

By the time John F. Kennedy became president of the United States in January 1961, the situation in South Vietnam was steadily deteriorating. Violence directed at Diem's government was rising dramatically. Between 1959 and 1961, the number of South Vietnamese government officials assassinated leaped from twelve hundred to four thousand per year. While Diem's government controlled Saigon and other cities in the south of the country, the Viet Cong dominated the rural areas. Although the government sent troops into villages by day in pursuit of the Communists, after the troops left at night the Viet Cong would return. Moreover, many South Vietnamese people considered Diem's government the enemy, a fact that even those close to Diem were aware of. "Except for the color of our skin, we are no different from the French,"[30] lamented one of Diem's aides.

Diem's position had already been weakened by an earlier peasant uprising against his government. On January 17, 1960, in the Ben Tre province, peasants armed with just machetes, spears, and sharpened sticks joined 162 Viet Cong troops equipped with only four rifles in an attack on government troops and officials. Despite having so few weapons, the group captured enough guns to arm an entire company, and used them to defeat a government counterattack.

Despite these problems, Kennedy initially tried to assure Diem of America's continued support. He replaced Durbrow as ambassador with Frederick Nolting, who

In an attempt to assure Diem of continued U.S. support, President Kennedy (pictured) assigned Frederick Nolting as ambassador to South Vietnam.

was a staunch Diem backer. In May 1961, Kennedy sent Vice President Lyndon Johnson to Saigon to consult with Diem in hopes of persuading him to be more amenable to U.S. advice.

But while he showered Diem with praise, Johnson, a master politician who thrived on one-on-one contact, returned

from South Vietnam uncertain if he had succeeded. He confided to an aide:

> I don't know about this fellow Diem. He was tickled as hell when I promised him forty million dollars and talked about military aid, but he turned deaf and dumb every time I talked about him speeding up and beefing up some health and welfare projects. I spent two hours and forty-five minutes with him; tried to get knee-to-knee and belly-to-belly so he wouldn't misunderstand me, but I don't know if I got to him.[31]

Despite his doubts, however, Johnson commented that "Diem's the only boy we got out there,"[32] and that sentiment continued to drive American policy in South Vietnam. To many in the U.S. government, Diem was preventing the rest of Southeast Asia from falling into Communist hands.

A Further Erosion of Support

It soon became apparent to American observers that Diem was not as firmly in charge of his nation as many had believed. In the fall of 1961, U.S. State Department employee William Jordan, on a mission to South Vietnam, noted that an alarmingly large number of soldiers, officials, and citizens had lost confidence in Diem.

Unhappiness with Diem among his compatriots publicly erupted again on February 27, 1962, when two South Vietnamese Air Force pilots tried to kill him and his brother Nhu by attacking the presidential palace. Yet instead of instituting reforms, Diem used this attack as an excuse to round up yet more political opponents and suspected Communist sympathizers.

Adding to South Vietnam's woes was that its army (Army of the Republic of Vietnam, or ARVN), despite massive American aid and advice, performed badly. In battle, the Viet Cong captured so many U.S.-supplied weapons that the Communists began counting on Diem and his troops as their best source of arms.

Instead of improving, the ARVN responded to increased American aid by becoming timid and reluctant to directly engage the enemy; they preferred to rely on U.S. air strikes and artillery to do the job for them. This followed Diem's directives; he ordered his officers to avoid casualties because for him, the army's main duty was to be ready to put down any coups against him.

Typical of the ARVN's lack of interest in fighting was the Battle of Ap Bac fought in January 1963. South Vietnamese troops outnumbered the Viet Cong forces by nearly ten to one, but ARVN commanders did not take advantage of their vast superiority in numbers. They refused to order their troops to advance against the enemy, who stood and fought from prepared defensive positions. The result was that the Viet Cong suffered just eighteen dead and thirty-nine wounded, while government losses were eighty dead and more than one hundred wounded. In response, U.S. senator Mike Mansfield remarked after visiting

Saigon that despite spending almost $2 billion, America's efforts to establish an independent South Vietnam were "not even at the beginning of a beginning."[33]

Buddhist Uprisings Bring Events to a Head

By early 1963 the goals and expectations of Diem and the United States were almost diametrically opposed. Diem felt that by demanding so much influence in his country, the United States was practicing the same brand of colonialism as had France. When Ambassador Nolting told Diem that "we [America] would expect to share in the decision-making process in the political, economic and military fields as they affect the security situation,"[34] the South Vietnamese president became annoyed. "Vietnam," he said pointedly, "did not want to be a protectorate."[35]

Events came to a head in the spring of 1963, and the flashpoint was the increasingly strained relationship between the Catholic Diem and the large Buddhist population in Vietnam. On May 8, a peaceful Buddhist rally against a government rule that forbade flying the flag of the World Fellowship of Buddhists ended tragically when ARVN soldiers killed eight demonstrators. The killings sparked antigovernment protests by Buddhists throughout South Vietnam. One of the leaders of the uprising was the monk Tri Quang, who told U.S. officials: "The United States must either make Diem reform or get rid of him. You are responsible for the present trouble

The killing of Buddhist demonstrators led to widespread rallies against the Diem regime.

but Diem ignored them. Instead he blamed the eight deaths on the Viet Cong. The crisis worsened on June 11, when an elderly Buddhist monk named Thich Quang Duc publicly immolated himself on a Saigon street. The next day, the grisly photo of the burning monk was on the front page of newspapers all over the world. Public opinion, both in the United States and elsewhere, turned against Diem's government.

Diem's brother Nhu further antagonized the United States when in a newspaper interview he advocated the withdrawal of half of the American military advisors in South Vietnam. Some in the U.S. government felt that Nhu's words were really those of Diem, and that this was Diem's way of trying to rid his country of Americans.

A New Ambassador Brings More Trouble for Diem

Relations between the United States and Vietnam were strained still more when on June 27, 1963, Kennedy named Henry Cabot Lodge as ambassador to South Vietnam, replacing Nolting. Unlike Nolting, Lodge did not like Diem. The ambassador now became one of the loudest voices among U.S. officials advocating Diem's replacement.

because you back Diem and his government of ignoramuses."[36]

The Buddhists demanded that those responsible for the killings be punished,

Further trouble erupted on August 21, when Nhu ordered armed raids on Buddhist pagodas in which more than fourteen hundred Buddhists were arrested. In response, demonstrations denouncing Diem rocked South Vietnam. The attack outraged American officials, who had counseled Diem to negotiate with the Buddhists. They realized that Diem no longer cared what they thought.

Lodge and others in the U.S. government now believed it was time to do more than talk about replacing Diem. Already in existence was a group of dissident South Vietnamese generals who wanted to topple the Diem regime, but who had restrained themselves for fear of the U.S. response. Lodge quietly let the group know that the United States would not interfere with their plans. On August 29, Lodge sent a cable to Washington that read, in part: "We are launched on a course from which there is no respectable turning back: the overthrow of the Diem government."[37]

Now Diem and his brother saw the danger they were in and took desperate measures to try and remain in power. With Saigon rife with rumors of American involvement in an impending takeover, Nhu secretly contacted the Communists to see if the two sides could come to an agreement ending the war by themselves.

Following the example of Thich Quang Duc, other Buddhist monks immolated themselves to protest Diem's actions.

Coup

But events were moving too quickly. On October 2, the United States suspended economic subsidies for South Vietnamese commercial imports, froze loans for developmental projects, and halted financial support for the government's Special Forces unit. These actions sent a prearranged signal to the dissident generals that the United States would not stop their planned coup.

Early in the morning of November 1, 1963, Lodge met with Diem at the presidential palace in Saigon. Diem complained about Americans conspiring against his government, but Lodge feigned ignorance. "Please tell President Kennedy that I am a good and frank ally,"[38] Diem told Lodge as their meeting ended.

A few hours later, the generals launched their coup. Under attack in the presidential palace, Diem called Lodge, saying that some units of his army were rebelling and asking, in effect, if the United States still supported him. Lodge, who had played a major role in encouraging the coup, replied that "I do not feel well enough informed to be able to tell you."[39]

On November 2, after a fruitless search for loyal military units to come to their aid, Diem and his brother Nhu surrendered to the rebels. Some officials in Washington, including President Kennedy, had assumed that the brothers would be given safe conduct out of the country once the coup was over. However, Diem and Nhu were loaded into an armored car with their hands tied behind their backs, driven to a remote location, and shot.

When news of the deaths reached Kennedy in the White House, he paled, jumped up in shock, and rushed out of the room. Later, with the president still depressed over the deaths, a friend tried to bolster his spirits by pointing out that Diem and Nhu had both been tyrants.

"No," said the president. "They were in a difficult position. They did the best they could for their country."[40]

Chapter 3

Lyndon B. Johnson

O n November 22, 1963, Lyndon B. Johnson became president of the United States upon the assassination of John F. Kennedy. One year later, Johnson was elected president in his own right, crushing Republican Barry Goldwater in one of the most lopsided presidential elections in American history.

Less than four years after his landslide victory, Johnson's enormous popularity had been completely destroyed by the Vietnam War. The once-popular president was a virtual prisoner in the White House, besieged by antiwar protesters and even rejected by members of his own party. Of all those who stumbled over Vietnam, Johnson's fall was one of the most dramatic.

A Political Family

Lyndon Baines Johnson was born on August 27, 1908, in a farmhouse in Gillespie County, Texas. He was the oldest of five children born to Sam, a farmer who had served in the Texas legislature, and Re- bekah, a former newspaper reporter.

In 1913, after his efforts at growing cotton failed, Sam Johnson moved his family to Johnson City, Texas, so that he could enter the real estate market. Four years later, Sam again won election to the Texas legislature. Sometimes he took Lyndon with him when he campaigned, giving his young son his first taste of politics. During his political career, Sam never lost an election.

Unfortunately, Sam Johnson was not as skilled at business as he was at politics. In addition to his real estate activities, Sam had assembled a large farm by buying adjacent land parcels from his relatives, often at inflated prices. Burdened with debt, Johnson fell deeper and deeper into financial difficulties. The more he struggled, the more he drank and the more he became depressed.

Eventually, under the strain of alcoholism and depression, Sam and Rebekah became emotionally estranged.

Lyndon B. Johnson is inaugurated as president of the United States after the assassination of John F. Kennedy.

This near-collapse of the family forced Lyndon, as the oldest child, to become a father figure to his four younger siblings.

A Brief Teaching Career

In 1924 Johnson graduated from high school, but was unable to attend college because he lacked some of the courses required of applicants. Disappointed, he went with some friends to California, where he found work as a clerk in a law office.

Johnson was determined to attend college, however. After returning home, early in 1927 Johnson took and passed all the courses he needed and was permitted to enroll in Southwest Texas State Teachers College, where he majored in history. Financial woes plagued Johnson, however. To earn tuition money, he took time out from his own studies for a nine-month period in 1928–1929 to teach seventh and eighth grades in an all-Hispanic school. Johnson's students were all poverty stricken, but his natural compassion for those less fortunate than himself came to the surface. He threw himself into the job with energy and enthusiasm.

In August 1930, Johnson graduated from Southwest Texas with a history degree. He taught for one month at a school in the town of Pearsall until his uncle George got him a job teaching speech at prestigious Sam Houston High School in Houston. However, as had been the case with his father, an interest in politics overrode all other concerns. So in late November 1931, Johnson seized an opportunity to go to Washington, D.C., as secretary to newly elected Democratic congressman Richard Kleberg.

Mr. Johnson Goes to Washington

In his new job Johnson learned the ins and outs of politics, attaching himself to Washington, D.C.'s power brokers, such as Speaker of the House of Representatives John Nance Garner and Majority Whip Sam Rayburn. From these savvy politicians, Johnson learned how to cultivate the right friends and influence the right people. As biographer Paul K. Conkin said: "At the end of three years . . . LBJ knew Washington as well as most senior congressmen."[41]

Johnson took another step forward in his political education in March 1933, when President Franklin D. Roosevelt took office and began implementing his New Deal, the federal programs designed to break the grip of the Great Depression and get the U.S. economy moving again. As new federal money poured out of Washington, Johnson kept Representative Kleberg's constituents abreast of everything that was occurring so that they would not miss a chance to take advantage of these opportunities. As Johnson saw the positive impact these federal programs had on people, he became a firm believer in the philosophy that government existed to help the average citizen. Furthermore, keeping in constant contact with the people back home made Johnson almost as well known as Kleberg himself.

Although he was working hard and planting the seeds of his own political career, Johnson was lonely. That situation changed in the summer of 1934, when he met Claudia Alta Taylor, a secretary at the Texas Railroad Commission Office in Austin, on a blind date. After a whirlwind courtship, on November 17, 1934, Johnson and Taylor were married. Johnson was delighted that, because his new wife was known by her childhood nickname of

the chance to become director of the National Youth Administration (NYA) for Texas in 1935. The NYA was a federal program that offered employment opportunities for youths in each state. Thanks to the superb organizational skills Johnson had developed while working for Kleberg, he soon had the best NYA program in the country. Even the president's wife, Eleanor Roosevelt, came to Austin and praised Johnson, who was the youngest NYA director in the country.

Congressman Johnson

Yet despite his success as an administrator, Johnson was intent on carving a name for himself as an elected official. That chance came in February 1937, due to the sudden death of Congressman James P. Buchanan, who had represented Johnson's home district. Although very young at age twenty-eight and

Lyndon B. Johnson married Claudia Alta Taylor (also known as "Lady Bird") on November 17, 1934.

unfamiliar to many voters, Johnson used ten thousand dollars that Lady Bird had inherited from her mother to launch a vigorous campaign for the vacant Congressional seat. The race attracted seven other candidates, but Johnson campaigned as a complete supporter of President Roosevelt's policies—the only one to do so. Johnson won the election, garnering three thousand more votes than his nearest competitor.

"Lady Bird," they both had the same initials "LBJ."

With his personal life in order, and feeling that he had learned all he could as Kleberg's secretary, Johnson jumped at

As a Democratic congressman, Johnson continued working strenuously on behalf of his constituents. Johnson's support for Roosevelt's programs led to a friendship with the president, and cashing in on that connection, Johnson obtained federal funds for building dams, highways, and other public improvement projects in his district. Thanks to his ability to bring federal projects and money to his district, he became known as a "can-do" congressman.

But although he enjoyed the House of Representatives, Johnson yearned for a more prestigious office. In April 1941, his opportunity arrived, again because of an untimely death, this time of Texas senator Morris Sheppard. Johnson mounted an aggressive campaign for the vacant seat, and at first his efforts seemed to pay off: Initial results put him thirteen thousand votes ahead in the special election to fill Sheppard's seat. For two days it seemed as if Johnson had won, but as more votes were counted the balance shifted in his opponent's favor. Johnson ended up losing by a razor-thin margin of thirteen hundred votes out of more than six hundred thousand cast.

Johnson returned to the House of Representatives, but not for long. That December, after the Japanese attack on Pearl Harbor plunged the United States into World War II, he was one of the first members of Congress to enter the military. But Johnson spent just a few months in the armed forces before returning to Washington, D.C., in the summer of 1942. By now

he was bored with the House of Representatives; the path to real power, such as Speaker of the House, was too long. Although his constituents considered him a good representative, he was unknown outside his own district. He was impatient to move forward, haunted by fears of an early death as had happened to his father at age sixty and his grandfather at age fifty-nine. (His personal habits—heavy smoking, drinking bouts, and binge eating—exacerbated those fears.) The allure of the House was further dimmed for Johnson by President Roosevelt's sudden death in April 1945. Not only did he feel he had lost a personal friend, but the president's death ended the easy access to power that he had enjoyed with Roosevelt in the White House.

Second Time Is the Charm

In 1948 Johnson got another opportunity to run for the Senate when incumbent senator Pappy O'Daniel retired. Again, the lead seesawed back and forth, but this time Johnson won—by just eighty-seven votes.

As a senator, Johnson wasted no time demonstrating his political acumen, and he moved quickly through the Democratic Party's leadership ranks. With his unrelenting capacity for hard work and enormous talents for personal persuasion, Johnson proved to be a master at striking compromises with other senators regardless of party or political philosophy. By 1955 he had become majority leader; no one had ever achieved that position so rapidly before. In his leadership role Johnson used his political skills to shepherd important legislation through Congress, most notably a civil rights bill in 1957 and the law establishing the National Aeronautics and Space Agency (NASA) in 1958.

Johnson's rapid advancement, however, came with a price. On July 2, 1955, he suffered a massive heart attack, and nearly died en route to the hospital. Under doctor's orders, Johnson gave up smoking and began watching his weight, but his illness reinforced his fears of an early death.

In spite of his close call, Johnson was viewed as a top prospect for higher political office. He had briefly been a candidate for the Democratic presidential nomination in 1956, and four years later, Johnson was considered one of the party's top prospects for the White House. But he took too long to declare his candidacy, and by the time he did, Massachusetts senator John F. Kennedy had sewn up the nomination.

As a senator, Johnson used his political skills to shepherd important legislation through Congress.

A Surprise Acceptance

Although some people thought that Johnson's political ascent had ended, Kennedy, in a surprise move, asked Johnson to be his running mate. Johnson then stunned many of his supporters by accepting the of-fer from his former rival. Although some historians today still wonder why the proud Johnson accepted the second spot, others feel that Johnson had simply tired of the Senate and was ready for a new challenge. In the November election, Kennedy and

Johnson won a narrow victory over the Republican ticket, headed by Richard Nixon.

Johnson quickly found that being vice president was a poor outlet for his energy and enthusiasm; he felt frustrated at his limited duties and lack of impact on national and world affairs. He had gone from being the master of the Senate and a broker of political deals to an advisor to the president with an almost ceremonial role in national affairs. Nevertheless, he was a loyal and trusted aide and advisor to Kennedy. The president, sensing Johnson's disillusionment, tried to keep him involved in the decision-making process, frequently sought his counsel on issues, and insisted that he attend meetings of the National Security Council.

With few official duties to occupy him, Johnson became a sort of roving ambassador. He would travel to foreign countries to meet their leaders and then give Kennedy his impressions of them. Of the nearly three dozen countries that he visited, perhaps none was as important to U.S. policy as South Vietnam. Sent there in May 1961 to convince President Ngo Dinh Diem to accept more American guidance in his country's affairs, Johnson was effusive in his public praise of Diem, calling him the "George Washington and Franklin Roosevelt"[42] of his country.

Privately, Johnson was more reserved. His report to Kennedy on South Vietnam advocated a three-year aid program to help the country establish its independence. The report also contained a prophetic warning:

If the Vietnamese government backed by a three-year liberal aid program cannot do this job, then we had better remember the experience of the French who wound up with several hundred thousand men in Vietnam and were still unable to do it.[43]

Johnson would soon need to heed his own advice.

On November 22, 1963, Johnson found himself vaulted to the nation's highest office when Kennedy was assassinated while on a visit to Dallas.

New President, Old Problems

As president, Johnson inherited the deteriorating situation in South Vietnam that had bedeviled Kennedy. The U.S.-endorsed coup that had overthrown Diem just three weeks before Kennedy's death had hurt rather than helped the country. The ruling council of generals that succeeded Diem constantly quarreled among themselves, leading to further domestic instability, and the ARVN (South Vietnamese army) continued losing ground to the Communists.

Johnson knew that his options in South Vietnam were limited: Continue aid at the present level and hope that things would improve; dramatically escalate the U.S. involvement to try and turn things around; or pull out entirely and almost certainly watch the country fall to the Communists. Johnson knew that none of these options were good. Moreover, he sensed that he had to make a choice. One evening, right

A U.S. helicopter delivers supplies to South Vietnamese troops. Johnson faced three questions about U.S. involvement in Vietnam: continue aid at present levels, escalate, or pull out.

after he became president, he said that because of Vietnam he had "the terrible feeling that something has grabbed me around the ankles and won't let go."[44]

Yet despite his doubts, Johnson continued Kennedy's policy toward Vietnam. Just two days after becoming president, Johnson dictated and signed an official National Security Council memorandum that said the United States would continue helping South Vietnam "win their contest against the externally directed and supported Communist conspiracy."[45] A believer in the Domino Theory, Johnson

proclaimed that he was not going to lose Vietnam and watch all of Southeast Asia become Communist.

Vietnam did not, however, consume all of Johnson's attention. The first two years of Johnson's presidency saw a staggering amount of important and far-reaching domestic legislation passed: more than one hundred new bills, including laws dealing with civil rights, health care (the establishment of Medicare and Medicaid), higher education, and poverty. These laws were all part of Johnson's Great Society program, and reflected his belief in the power of the government to help people.

President in His Own Right

Johnson used the huge public support he received as the successor to the martyred Kennedy to push many of his programs through Congress. Johnson's overwhelming victory over Republican Barry Goldwater in the 1964 presidential election, in which he received 61 percent of the popular vote and won all but six states, provided further legislative fuel for his domestic political agenda.

Yet the election victory had come with a price that was unknown to the American public at the time. The United States had been conducting spy missions along North Vietnam's coast when on August 2, 1964, in the midst of the campaign between Johnson and Goldwater, the American destroyer USS *Maddox* was attacked by three North Vietnamese patrol boats. (Whether or not the *Maddox* was in international waters at the time is a matter of dispute, since North Vietnam had never officially defined their territorial waters.)

On August 4, the *Maddox* and a second U.S. destroyer, *Turner Joy,* reported a possible torpedo attack, although a visual sighting of the torpedoes was never confirmed.

In his campaign Goldwater had been calling for tougher military measures in South Vietnam, including an extensive use of U.S. air power, and Johnson knew that he could not afford to look weak by comparison. For this reason, on August 5, he ordered retaliatory bombing raids against North Vietnam, even though there was scant evidence that the torpedo attack had actually occurred. Two days later, at Johnson's request, the U.S. Congress passed the Gulf of Tonkin Resolution, which gave him the authority to take all necessary measures to protect U.S. forces and to prevent more aggression by the Communists—in effect, blanket approval to wage war in Vietnam. Thus Johnson was free to escalate the U.S. involvement in South Vietnam without further congressional approval. He would use this freedom often over the next few years to build up the American military presence to more than five hundred thousand troops.

Initially, however, Johnson tried to downplay the situation in Vietnam, particularly after his win over Goldwater. He continually rejected suggestions from his military advisors to extensively bomb North Vietnam, call up the reserves, and virtually put the country on a war footing. Johnson was worried that a full-scale conflict would scuttle his Great Society programs by diverting time, money, and attention to the war. Yet Johnson was also determined to stop what he considered Communist aggression in Vietnam. Thus he tried to keep the focus on his domestic

programs, while keeping the war in the background as much as possible. Johnson described his dilemma in characteristically earthy terms: "I knew from the start that I was bound to be crucified either way I moved," he later said.

> If I left the woman I really loved—the Great Society—in order to get involved with that bitch of a war on the other side of the world, then I would lose everything at home. All my programs. . . . But if I left that war and let the Communists take over South Vietnam, then I would be seen as a coward and my nation would be seen as an ap-

Worried about ruining his Great Society programs, Johnson at first rejected advice to bomb North Vietnam.

peaser and we would both find it impossible to accomplish anything for anybody anywhere on the entire globe.[46]

The Die Is Cast

But in spite of the aid that Johnson obtained for the country, by 1965 the situation in South Vietnam was still unstable. The country's government had been revamped seven times in 1964 and then twice more early in 1965. Concerned that South Vietnam was on the verge of falling to the Communists, in February Johnson initiated a bombing campaign against North Vietnam and also sent two U.S. Marine battalions to South Vietnam—the first U.S. combat troops to enter the country. Yet the ARVN continued to perform poorly, forcing General William Westmoreland, commander of the American forces in South Vietnam, to ask for more American troops to turn the tide.

Desperately Johnson searched for alternatives. He had campaigned for election in 1964 on a pledge not to send Americans to do the fighting for the South Vietnamese, but now he was dangerously close to doing just that. Still seeking to keep the fighting in South Vietnam out of the public eye, Johnson increased American troop strength little by little in the first half of 1965. He also tried to influence North Vietnam, offering a $1-billion economic redevelopment plan for Southeast Asia in return for a negotiated settlement to the war. "Old Ho can't turn that down,"[47] Johnson said at the time. But North Vietnamese leader Ho Chi Minh did.

Privately, Johnson fretted to aides about the American military's desire for him to escalate the conflict and what might happen if he did. "They're trying to get me in a war over there. It will destroy me."[48] Yet he also knew that he would be ruined politically if he allowed South Vietnam to fall to the Communists. In mid-June, Westmoreland requested that American troop

strength be more than doubled to stave off South Vietnam's collapse. Seeing no alternative, Johnson announced on July 28, 1965, that he was sending fifty thousand more American troops to Vietnam, with more to come if needed. Sending American boys off to war was, said Johnson, a "most agonizing and painful duty."[49]

Johnson was gambling that more men and increased bombing would quickly turn the tide in South Vietnam without jeopardizing his Great Society programs. But as he had feared, the North Vietnamese merely matched the increased U.S. troop presence, causing Westmoreland to continually ask for more soldiers in turn. As a result, the American military presence in Vietnam soared from 75,000 to 125,000 in August 1965, and to almost 200,000 by year's end. By then, Westmoreland was estimating that he might need as many as 600,000 men by the end of 1967.

The bombing campaign against North Vietnam also turned out to have little effect. Instead of destroying the North Vietnamese's will to fight, all it did was unite the populace and increase their determination to resist. Years later, a North Vietnamese physician spoke about the effect of the bombing: "The Americans thought that the more bombs they dropped, the quicker we would fall to our knees and surrender. But the bombs heightened rather than dampened our spirit."[50]

By the end of 1965, the military buildup, coupled with Johnson's increased domestic spending, was causing inflationary pressure on the U.S. economy. Some advisors urged the president to increase taxes and scale back his Great Society programs to slow the economy and reduce inflation, but Johnson refused. Taking those steps would be a public admission of the war's growing impact, and Johnson still hoped to keep Vietnam out of the American public's consciousness.

Anger Builds over the War

But the public was well aware of the war in Vietnam. More than thirty-six thousand men had gotten draft notices in the autumn of 1965, the most since the height of the Korean War. Marches and other demonstrations against the war were becoming commonplace. Approximately thirty thousand antiwar protesters descended on Washington on November 27, 1965, raising a cry that would soon become familiar: "Hey, hey, L.B.J., how many kids did you kill today?"[51]

Desperately Johnson searched for a way to end the war. In December 1965, he halted the bombing of North Vietnam,

A group of U.S. troops arrives in the field. The buildup in Vietnam soon put inflationary pressure on the U.S. economy, making the war a difficult issue to ignore.

hoping it would bring Hanoi to the bargaining table, but it was a futile gesture, since the positions of the combatants were irreconcilable. The Communists considered South Vietnam's government illegitimate and wanted it removed; the United States had no intention of abandoning its ally. The vast gap between those two positions made negotiations hopeless.

As the war demanded more attention, time, money, and personnel, it drained the impetus from Johnson's Great Society programs. As presidential aide Jack Valenti recalled:

> Vietnam was a fungus, slowly spreading its suffocating crust over the great plans of the president, both here and overseas. No matter what we turned our hands and minds to, there was Vietnam, its contagion infecting everything that it touched, and it seemed to touch everything.[52]

Ultimately the war could no longer be swept under the political rug. From July 1966 to June 1967, the war cost $21 billion, and the money had to be found somewhere. In August 1967, Johnson reluctantly proposed a 10 percent surcharge on individual and corporate income taxes as a way to prevent inflation by lowering consumers' spending and generate money for the war, but Congress delayed action on the measure for a year. Without the necessary funds to pay for the war, the budget deficit shot up from $10 billion to $30 billion for fiscal 1968, which in turn set off ruinous inflation of prices.

By now the president who had been reelected in a landslide just a few years earlier was rapidly losing public support. In June 1966, Johnson's approval rating fell below 50 percent. The following year, another survey revealed that for the first time, more people felt that the American commitment to Vietnam was a mistake rather than the right thing to do. An increasing number of Americans blamed that mistake on Johnson.

Johnson was also losing support for the war within his administration. Secretary of Defense Robert McNamara, who had masterminded the buildup of U.S. soldiers and materials in South Vietnam in the firm belief that it would bring victory, realized by the fall of 1965 that he had miscalculated. As Johnson biographer Paul Conkin wrote: "Horrified by the costs and the cruelty of the expanding war and swayed by the critics, he suffered from a devastating ambivalence."[53] Other presidential advisors also had growing doubts that America could achieve military success in Vietnam.

Stalemate

Johnson kept looking for light at the end of the tunnel, but the news from Vietnam only got worse. Early in 1967, a Central Intelligence Agency (CIA) report about the air war dismayed Johnson. It revealed that he had been escalating the bombing campaign against North Vietnam for eighteen months with almost no effect. Hundreds of bridges had been destroyed, but nearly all had been rebuilt or bypassed. Thousands of vehicles had been wrecked, but North Vietnamese traffic continued to flow smoothly. Approximately 75 percent of the country's oil storage facilities had been destroyed, yet no fuel shortage had occurred.

The ground war was going no better. With about 470,000 troops in Vietnam, Westmoreland said he could do "little better than hold our own."[54] When he requested more troops, Johnson asked: "When we add divisions, can't the enemy add divisions, and if so, where does it end?"[55] The general had no answer to his question, and Johnson already knew how unpopular he had become with voters as more and more of their sons were drafted and sent to Vietnam.

Yet the political cost was not the only reason that Johnson hesitated to send in more troops. He was also concerned that a dramatic escalation by the United States would cause Communist China, one of Hanoi's allies and a country that bordered North Vietnam, to enter the war on North Vietnam's side. Johnson was plagued by images of hundreds of thousands of Chinese Communist troops pouring into Vietnam, just as they did in Korea in the previous decade.

Throughout 1967, Johnson followed two divergent paths in Vietnam: He gradually escalated the bombing campaign while also seeking peace. In June he met with Alexey Kosygin, premier of the Soviet Union, in a historic summit meeting at Glassboro, New Jersey. Johnson wanted Kosygin to pressure Hanoi to begin peace negotiations, but the effort failed because Russian influence with the North Vietnamese was not as great as the president had imagined.

By the end of 1967, Johnson was unwilling to go out of the White House because of the antiwar protests. He looked exhausted: his face was ashen, his eyes were sunken, and his skin was flabby. Yet he had reason to be hopeful on Vietnam: The increased American military presence seemed to have the Viet Cong in retreat, enabling more of South Vietnam to be free of Communist control than at any time in the last few years. Even Westmoreland joined in the optimism during a brief November return to the United States, claiming that the end of the war was coming into view.

The Tet Offensive Changes Everything

Buoyed by these optimistic assessments, the American public was caught off-guard when the Viet Cong launched their massive Tet Offensive throughout South Vietnam on January 31, 1968. Although the campaign ended with large casualties for the Communists, the fact that they could mount such an offensive clearly contradicted the image Johnson and Westmoreland had portrayed of a defeated, discouraged foe.

The Tet Offensive also affected a group of elder political leaders nicknamed the "Wise Men"—including General Omar Bradley, General Matthew Ridgeway, and

Smoke and wreckage fill the streets of Saigon during the Tet Offensive. Discouraged by the attack, many statesmen and politicians began to turn against the war.

former Treasury Secretary Douglas Dillon—that Johnson called upon periodically to discuss administration policy. Although just five months earlier they had endorsed U.S. policy in Vietnam, by late March 1968, almost all of them had turned against the war. The implications of this change of heart were not lost on Johnson. As he later wrote: "If they had been so deeply influenced by the reports of the Tet offensive, what must the average citizen be thinking?"[56]

Johnson was besieged on all sides. His senior aides were growing more pessimistic about the war, his pleas for new domestic programs were falling on deaf ears in Congress, and riots and antiwar demonstrations were ravaging the country. Then came the final straw: Johnson nearly lost the New Hampshire presidential primary in February to Senator Eugene McCarthy, who had made opposition to the war the centerpiece of his campaign.

Johnson Bows Out

Johnson had had enough. In a televised speech on March 31, 1968, he announced that he was restricting U.S. air strikes on North Vietnam as a means of jump-starting peace negotiations. Then he dropped a bombshell announcement: "I shall not seek, and I will not accept, the nomination of my party for another term as your President."[57]

The last ten months of his presidential term were anything but pleasant for Johnson. In April 1968, Dr. Martin Luther King Jr. was assassinated, sparking still more domestic violence. Two months later, Robert Kennedy, brother of John F. Kennedy, was also assassinated while campaigning for the presidency. In May, peace talks between the United States and North Vietnam had begun in Paris, but quickly deadlocked. Later that summer, antiwar protests and violence marred the Democratic National Convention in Chicago.

In January 1969, during his last State of the Union address to Congress, Johnson said: "Now, it is time to leave. I hope it may be said, a hundred years from now, that by working together we helped to make our country more just, more just for all of its people. . . . "[58]

Lyndon Johnson did indeed try to improve his country. Unfortunately, the president who sought to make his mark on American society through innovative and pioneering domestic programs instead found his legacy defined by a war in a country thousands of miles away. After he left office Johnson returned to his ranch in Texas, where he faded from public view. He grew his hair to his shoulders, resumed eating and smoking indiscriminately, and managed the affairs of his ranch just as he had managed his presidency with staff conferences and written memos. Just four years after leaving the presidency Johnson's heart gave out and he died on January 22, 1973.

Chapter 4

William Westmoreland

From 1964 to 1968, General William C. Westmoreland was in command of U.S. troops in Vietnam. His accomplishments during these four years included stopping the Communists' military progress, stabilizing South Vietnam's army, and winning numerous victories against a wily and persistent foe. Yet despite these achievements, Westmoreland could not defeat the Communists and returned to the United States amid withering criticism over his conduct of the war.

An Affinity for Uniforms

William Childs Westmoreland was born on March 26, 1914 in Saxon, South Carolina. His father was James Ripley ("Rip") Westmoreland, a textile mill manager, and his mother was Eugenia Talley ("Mimi") Childs.

Although he had attended the Citadel, South Carolina's famed military college, Rip Westmoreland always wanted to be a lawyer. Instead, he wound up in business.

Nevertheless, he still hoped that his son would be a lawyer. His wife, however, wanted her child to be a doctor.

General William C. Westmoreland, commander of U.S. forces in South Vietnam.

But the boy had other ideas. Enamored of uniforms at an early age, William joined the Boy Scouts, and immediately took to the self-discipline and necessity for learning new skills. He also proved to be a natural leader: Once, on a camping trip, he threw a Cub Scout into a nearby creek when William thought the other boy was not paying enough attention to a lecture he was giving. Instead of hating him for it, the boy became one of Westmoreland's most devoted followers.

In June 1929, Westmoreland attended an international Scout jamboree in Great Britain. He combined it with a leisurely trip through Europe and discovered that he enjoyed traveling. Analyzing his future career options, Westmoreland decided that the only way to have everything that he wanted—a structured life, uniforms, and travel—was a military career. Consequently, upon graduation from high school in June 1931, he applied to the Citadel. After one year there, Westmoreland was considered the top cadet in the school because of his mastery of military skills such as character, command presence, and precision in drill.

West Point

His Citadel achievements made Westmoreland a prime candidate for an appointment to a military academy, and he entered the U.S. Military Academy at West Point in July 1932. Just as he had done at the Citadel, Westmoreland quickly established himself as one of the school's top students. His integrity, sense of fairness, and maturity, combined with his leadership qualities and his near-perfect grasp of his military duties, caught the attention of his superiors. By his senior year, Westmoreland had been named first captain, the highest rank a West Point cadet could attain. When he graduated in June 1936, Westmoreland received the coveted Pershing Sword as the cadet who had exhibited the greatest military proficiency.

When Westmoreland received his commission as a second lieutenant, the United States Army was just the eighteenth largest in the world, but things were about to change dramatically. Other parts of the globe were erupting into warfare: Italy had invaded Ethiopia in 1935 and Japan had invaded China in 1937. It seemed doubtful that America would be able to avoid the scourge of war that was sweeping across the world. Then on September 1, 1939, Germany invaded Poland, plunging Europe into the maelstrom of World War II.

War

For Westmoreland and the rest of the American military, war came a little more than two years later, when the Japanese bombed the American naval base at Pearl Harbor, Hawaii, on December 7, 1941. The attack jolted America's slow-motion military machine into high gear. Practically overnight, trainloads of draftees began piling into posts like Fort Bragg, where Westmoreland was stationed. In the rush to expand America's armed forces, Westmoreland was quickly promoted from captain to major—a rank that might have taken him fifteen years to achieve during peacetime—and given command of the 34th Artillery Battalion. After another promotion to lieutenant colonel, Westmoreland was sent into combat in North Africa late in 1942.

During the Battle of Kasserine Pass early in 1943, Westmoreland's unit played a critical role in stopping the Germans from expelling Allied troops from North Africa. Westmoreland's battalion received a Presidential Unit Citation for their efforts, and Westmoreland's command abilities again caught the attention of his superiors.

The Rocket List

After the fighting in North Africa was over, Westmoreland was sent to Europe. He remained in combat until the war in Europe was over in May 1945, receiving the Legion of Merit and the Bronze Star for his actions under fire. Thanks to his excellent performance in combat, Westmoreland found himself after the war on a "rocket list" of promising young officers destined to go places within the army.

Westmoreland found further opportunity for advancement when in June 1950 North Korea

launched an invasion of South Korea, and the United States found itself in another major war. During the Korean conflict, Westmoreland commanded the 187th

The artillery battalion under Westmoreland's command received a Presidential Unit Citation for its efforts in the Battle of Kasserine Pass.

Airborne Regimental Combat Team. Although he saw little combat, in August 1952, he was promoted to brigadier general, one of the youngest generals in the U.S. Army.

As a young military leader, for several years in the mid-1950s, Westmoreland was posted to the Pentagon in Washington, D.C., serving in a variety of assignments. It was there that he began hearing about Vietnam, where France was struggling to maintain its colonial empire in a war against nationalist/Communist forces.

In 1956 Westmoreland, still on the "rocket list," was promoted again, this time becoming the army's youngest major general, and given command of the Army's 101st Airborne Division.

Other prestigious assignments followed. Four years after becoming major general, he was named superintendent of the Army's Military Academy at West Point. Both this appointment and the previous one were due to the influence of General Maxwell Taylor, who was the Army chief of staff and who had taken a liking to Westmoreland.

Return to West Point

The West Point assignment delighted Westmoreland, as he later wrote in his autobiography *A Soldier Reports:*

Aside from my pleasure at returning to a place I loved and respected, I was anxious to carry on the good work of my predecessor, Lieutenant General Garrison Davidson, in modernizing an educational institution that I consider vital to an effective United States Army.[59]

By all accounts, Westmoreland was an excellent superintendent. Convinced that the next war would be fought using guerrilla-style tactics, he instituted a counterinsurgency warfare training program at West Point. At this time counterinsurgency warfare was brand new, and Westmoreland became an expert in the field.

This expertise would soon come in handy for Westmoreland. Always a keen observer of world events as they related to the U.S. military, he had watched the situation in Vietnam carefully and knew that his background fit the type of limited, guerrilla-style warfare that was being waged in that Southeast Asian country. "Throughout my days as superintendent [of West Point]," he wrote in *A Soldier Reports*, "I had an intuitive feeling that eventually I would go to Vietnam."[60]

At that time, in the early 1960s, the situation in South Vietnam was steadily deteriorating. The government's troops were unable to hold their ground against the forces of the Viet Cong. In December 1963, U.S. Secretary of Defense Robert S. McNamara went to the South Vietnamese capital of Saigon to assess the war effort. When he returned, he told President Lyndon Johnson that unless things changed drastically, South Vietnam would soon fall to the Communists.

A group of guerrillas undergoes marksmanship training. The Viet Cong became so skilled at guerrilla warfare that the South Vietnamese army was no match for them.

Among the changes that McNamara recommended was replacing General Paul Harkins, who was commander of the United States Military Assistance Command—Vietnam (USMACV). USMACV's role was to help the South Vietnamese defeat the Viet Cong and remain independent of its Communist neighbor, North Vietnam.

To Vietnam

Westmoreland, thanks to his excellent reputation and counterinsurgency background, seemed the logical choice to take over USMACV. In January 1964, he received orders to report to Vietnam as second in command to Harkins, with the prospect of replacing him in several months, once he became familiar with the situation.

Upon his arrival, Westmoreland found South Vietnam in chaos. The November 1963 coup that had ousted President Ngo Dinh Diem had brought not order but even more confusion, and rumors of another coup were rampant. Strikes by workers and students were crippling the country. To make matters worse, the ARVN (South Vietnamese army), despite years of assistance from the United States was, as Westmoreland later said, "poorly trained and poorly led."[61]

Just four days after Westmoreland's arrival in South Vietnam, another coup occurred, but it did nothing to stem the turmoil in the country. Westmoreland was, as he told a friend, "amazed and depressed"[62] by what he saw in South Vietnam.

Adding to Westmoreland's despair was that the American ambassador to South Vietnam, Henry Cabot Lodge, thought the country was on the verge of collapse. Lodge told the general that he had unsuccessfully tried to find the means "to hold together the South Vietnamese political patchwork."[63] Lodge was so convinced that Vietnam was on the brink of anarchy that he advised Westmoreland to establish a coastal sanctuary to which Americans could flee and be evacuated by U.S. ships when—not if—the country fell apart.

A Bottomless Pit

Two months later, when McNamara returned to South Vietnam to again personally assess the country's situation, Westmoreland was no more optimistic. The general told McNamara that Vietnam was a "bottomless pit"[64] in which the United States faced an enormous military challenge.

"I was convinced from the first that there were no easy solutions, that the war would be long and costly . . . that it would take a lot of resources and infinite patience on the part of the American people,"[65] Westmoreland later wrote.

Westmoreland was also becoming alarmed at the changing tactics of the Viet Cong. Instead of striking and then melting into the jungle in guerrilla style, the Viet Cong won a decisive battle at Binh Gia in late December 1964 by fighting in a con-

A wounded soldier is evacuated from a battlefield. General Westmoreland was not optimistic about the situation in South Vietnam.

ventional style and remaining on the battle-field after the initial contact. Schooled as he was in counterinsurgency warfare and Communist doctrine, Westmoreland knew this meant that the Viet Cong were moving into a mode of fighting designed to deliver a knockout blow via large, sustained attacks. Considering the sorry state of South Vietnam's armed forces at the time, Westmoreland was worried that these attacks would overwhelm them and enable the Communists to seize control of the country.

Yet there was little Westmoreland could do to turn the tide. The ARVN was reeling, so action by that force was out of the question, and Westmoreland's other military option—bombing by U.S. planes—also carried risks.

Bombing Begins

For months, President Johnson's military advisors had been pressuring him to authorize sustained bombing raids on North Vietnam so as to reduce the flow of military aid to the Viet Cong. But Westmoreland was not among the bombing advocates. He felt that taking more aggressive steps might cause North Vietnam to step up their attacks, which would be a disaster given the deplorable condition of the ARVN at the time.

Yet despite Westmoreland's misgivings, a bombing campaign against North Vietnam was initiated on March 2, 1965. The campaign was graduated, meaning that it increased in intensity and severity over time, and this added to Westmoreland's concerns. He considered a graduated

bombing campaign a serious mistake, because it enabled North Vietnam to gradually increase their tolerance to the attacks. He recalled:

> To my knowledge, the history of warfare contained no precedent for such a policy. In almost all wars the tempo of operations has gradually increased, but not through any conscious policy of gradual escalation, [but] rather through the gradually increasing availability of means. Faced with escalating pressure, the North Vietnamese could adapt to each new step and absorb the damage, so that any hope that the enemy's leaders would find the prospect of the next step unbearable would be false.[66]

Instead of wave after wave of bombers attacking dozens of targets, the bombing runs usually consisted of only two to four attacks per week by a few dozen planes. "That seemed to me a woefully weak way to send a message,"[67] Westmoreland later wrote.

American Troops Arrive

However, the bombing did have dramatic and long-term consequences. In planning for the campaign, which was to be based at the airfield at Da Nang, Westmoreland realized that the South Vietnamese would be unable to defend the location. To provide adequate defense and security, he requested that two battalions of U.S. marines be stationed at Da Nang. This request was approved, and the Marines landed there on February 26, 1965. Although their arrival was supposed to be low-key, girls waving welcome signs and carrying garlands of flowers greeted them.

These two battalions were the first U.S. ground combat troops in South Vietnam. From this innocuous beginning, the American military presence would ultimately mushroom to nearly 550,000 troops. Yet Westmoreland did not view these two battalions as the beginning of a massive buildup of U.S. forces in Vietnam. "I saw my call for marines at Da Nang not as a first step in a growing American commitment but as what I said at the time it was: a way to

secure a vital airfield and the air units using it . . ."[68] he recalled.

But as the war continued going badly for the ARVN, Westmoreland concluded that it would take at least one year to strengthen the South Vietnamese army to the point at which it could hold its own in battle against the Communists. In the meantime, he saw no alternative but the introduction of more U.S. troops to prevent the Communists from overrunning South Vietnam.

Pictured is the grave of an ARVN soldier. In order to prevent the total defeat of the ARVN, General Westmoreland requested more troops be sent to Vietnam.

Yet even with the addition of American troops, Westmoreland saw no quick victory, but rather, a long, bloody war. "Sizable American forces meant sizable American sacrifices, wounds, and deaths, probably extending over a long period of time, not months but years,"[69] he later wrote.

The amount of troops that Westmoreland wanted was indeed substantial: thirty- four American battalions and ten from America's ally, South Korea, for a total of 180,000 men. When President Johnson asked him whether the forty-four total battalions would be enough to defeat the Communists, Westmoreland answered they would not. He saw these troops as merely leveling the playing field against the enemy.

Westmoreland's troop request hit Washington like a bombshell. Approval meant involving America in a major land war in Southeast Asia, but denial meant, in the opinion of many, losing South Vietnam to the Communists. While Johnson and his advisors wrestled with the momentous decision, the Communists stepped up their attacks in South Vietnam. Trying to hold the line, on June 27, Westmoreland initiated the first American offensive operations of the war.

With American troops now on the offensive, Johnson had to either support them with additional military forces or else pull the soldiers out entirely—an unacceptable option to him. With little choice left, on July 28, 1965, Johnson announced that American fighting strength in Vietnam would be immediately increased from 75,000 to 125,000.

A Three-Phase War

With additional U.S. troops on the way, Westmoreland envisioned a three-phase war. Phase one, which he hoped would be over by the end of 1965, was to simply maintain the military status quo and help prevent more ARVN defeats. Phase two featured American-led forces taking the offensive against the enemy in high-priority areas near important towns and military installations. In the final phase, Westmoreland planned to attack and defeat the main body of enemy troops. He estimated that this phase would take between twelve and eighteen months after the conclusion of phase two. Yet even before he put his plan into effect, Westmoreland warned his superiors that he was going to need yet more troops to begin the final phase of his strategy.

Initially, Westmoreland's tactics achieved the desired result. The Viet Cong, used to dealing with the ARVN, were unprepared for the vastly superior firepower and competence of the American forces. Even the soldiers of the North Vietnamese Army (NVA), who were more professional and better organized than the Viet Cong guerrillas, found themselves outmatched by the United States.

One of Westmoreland's most effective combat weapons was air power. American planes would often bomb enemy positions before their troops even entered a fight, inflicting tremendous casualties. For example, during a one-month battle in November 1965 around the South Vietnamese river, Ia Drang, Communist forces suffered over three thousand killed, while the United States lost three hundred soldiers. Thanks in part to his generalship at Ia Drang, Westmoreland was named *Time* magazine's 1965 "Man of the Year."

But as significant as this and other victories were in stopping Communist advances in South Vietnam, Westmoreland knew from intelligence reports that the Communists, rather than being discouraged that they were now facing the United States, were actually increasing their troop strength in South Vietnam. Realizing that the war was a long way from being over, Westmoreland told McNamara that he was going to need two hundred thousand more troops in 1966, and possibly another two hundred thousand early the following year. At a conference in Honolulu in early February 1966, he repeated his belief to President Johnson and others in attendance that the war was going to last several years.

His belief that the war would be a long one notwithstanding, Westmoreland was convinced that phase one of his strategy had been successfully concluded. Through-

U.S. soldiers walk amongst dead Communist troops after the Battle of Ia Drang.

out most of 1966, therefore, Westmoreland employed phase two, targeting high-priority areas for offensive action. He knew that he could not expel enemy troops from South Vietnam and keep them out. Lacking sufficient personnel to guard the entire 900-

mile-long border of South Vietnam, Westmoreland chose to fight a war of attrition, in which the enemy would lose troops faster than they could be replenished, rather than one of territorial gain. He hoped that in the face of suffering heavy losses, the enemy might lose its desire to continue fighting.

Exploiting U.S. superiority in firepower and the mobility gained by using helicopters to move troops into battle, Westmoreland won repeated victories over the Viet Cong and North Vietnamese by searching out and destroying concentrations of enemy troops. Yet despite his success, in October 1966, Westmoreland admitted to Johnson that it was still impossible to predict when the war would end.

Unhappiness Spreads at Home

By now, the antiwar movement in the United States was growing, and as U.S. commander Westmoreland was one of its most visible targets. Protesters labeled him a murderer and a war criminal. This jolted Westmoreland, despite his claims to the contrary. "The antiwar movement was alien to him. . . . He did not understand it," said one of his former staff officers.

When he went to Vietnam, he had imagined himself as another Eisenhower. [He would] win the war and come back to a ticker-tape parade. Only it did not work out that way. Instead, he found himself knee-deep in a nasty little war of attrition. He wanted

to be a hero and instead he found himself being vilified.[70]

Westmoreland knew that his search-and-destroy strategy would probably not bring victory. He repeatedly urged the president and other government officials to expand the war by letting him attack enemy bases in neighboring Laos and Cambodia. But fears in Washington that these actions would cause China to enter the war on North Vietnam's behalf caused his requests to fall on deaf ears.

By early 1967, the war had become increasingly unpopular at home, as scholars, journalists, politicians and others joined the antiwar movement. There was a growing feeling throughout the country that the war was a stalemate, despite Westmoreland's success in producing enemy casualty rates ten to fifteen times higher than those for American troops. Westmoreland was concerned about the effect the antiwar sentiment was having on the morale of his troops. While briefly back in the United States, Westmoreland said that both he and his troops were dismayed by the antiwar protests. This remark sparked howls of indignation from newspapers such as the *Chicago Daily News*, which expressed the belief that he was trying to stifle legitimate criticism of the war.

Maintaining the Status Quo

As for the war itself, despite the continuing U.S. commitment of troops and materials, enemy troops continued to infiltrate South

Vietnam from the north at the rate of approximately seven thousand per month. To maintain the status quo, in April 1967, Westmoreland told Johnson that he needed at least one hundred thousand and possibly two hundred thousand more troops. When Johnson asked if the enemy simply could not just add divisions as well and wondered if there would ever be an end to the escalation, Westmoreland had no satisfactory answer.

Westmoreland's call for two hundred thousand more troops marked a turning point in the U.S. war effort. Stunned by the number, Johnson began looking for ways to achieve American goals in Vietnam that

did not require continually supplying more U.S. soldiers. While the president did eventually authorize 47,000 more troops for Westmoreland (bringing total American military strength up to 525,000), the drastic reduction in the number Westmoreland requested for South Vietnam signaled the president's search for a new strategy.

As part of that strategy, Johnson named General Creighton Abrams as Westmoreland's deputy commander and gave him the task of energizing the ARVN and getting it

In order to maintain the status quo, General Westmoreland continually requested more U.S. troops be sent to Vietnam.

more involved in combat operations—a process called Vietnamization. Because of his low opinion of the ARVN, Westmoreland had relegated it to a secondary role. It was Abrams's job to change that.

Although the leadership in Washington was clearly turning away from his search-and-destroy strategy, Westmoreland continued to request additional U.S. forces. After a series of military victories in mid-1967, he again pressed Secretary of Defense McNamara for two hundred thousand more troops, saying that the war "is not a stalemate. We are winning slowly but steadily."[71] Now was the time, he urged, to send more troops into South Vietnam and really knock the enemy back on his heels.

False Hope

Although he did not get the additional soldiers, Westmoreland felt that a turning point had been reached in Vietnam. He publicly expressed this feeling during a speech before the National Press Club in Washington, D.C., in November 1967. After reviewing his tenure as USMACV commander, Westmoreland said: "We have reached an important point when the end begins to come into view."[72]

The comment generated a flurry of favorable public opinion throughout the United States and raised the hope of many anxious families with sons or daughters serving in Vietnam that their children might be home soon.

Lulled into a false sense of security, the American public was totally unprepared for the events that began in the early morning hours of January 31, 1968, during the Vietnamese holiday of Tet, which celebrates the beginning of the lunar new year. A mostly Viet Cong force numbering eighty-four thousand troops launched a devastating series of coordinated attacks throughout South Vietnam. Thirty-six of the country's provincial capitals, 5 of its 6 autonomous cities, 64 of its 242 district capitals, and 50 of its hamlets were subjected to a furious assault by Communist troops that many Americans had believed were close to defeat.

The ferocity of the attacks stunned and shocked many Americans who had thought that the war was winding down. In reality, the Tet offensive accomplished little of military significance for the Communists, as Westmoreland was quick to point out. They lost more than thirty-seven thousand troops to approximately three thousand for the Americans and South Vietnamese, did not gain any territory, and failed to ignite a general uprising among the South Vietnamese people.

Where the Communists triumphed, however, was on the battlefield of U.S. public opinion. The strength of the Communist attack made it seem to many Americans that Westmoreland's war of attrition was a failure. As *Newsweek* editorialized, his strategy "had run into a dead end," and only the "deluded can console themselves with the comforting feeling that suddenly the war will turn the corner."[73] There was also concern that the Tet offensive caught U.S. forces unprepared.

Personal attacks on Westmoreland increased. He was denounced in Congress, savaged in the press, and ridiculed for his optimistic statements of just a few months before. Pulitzer-Prize-winning historian Arthur M. Schlesinger called him "our most disastrous general since Custer."[74]

Called Home

No commander could long survive in the face of such withering criticism. On March 23, 1968, President Johnson announced that in July Westmoreland would return to Washington to become Army chief of staff and that Abrams would replace him as USMACV commander. Although it is un-

clear whether he was recalled because of unhappiness over the war or whether it was a move long planned, what was certain was that Westmoreland was leaving Vietnam without the victory he craved.

For just over four years, Westmoreland served as the Army chief of staff. Following his retirement from the army, Westmoreland decided to enter politics and ran for the Republican nomination for governor of South Carolina in 1974. He proved to be

The victim of criticism and ridicule, Westmoreland (second from left) soon found himself back in Washington, D.C., and was appointed Army chief of staff.

a poor candidate, however, inept at making small talk and uncomfortable with the relatively unstructured nature of political campaigning. Although he began his campaign in the lead, he was actually glad when he lost the primary, admitting that he enjoyed a more regimented lifestyle than politics afforded.

Despite his defeat, Westmoreland was not long out of the public eye. In 1982 Westmoreland filed a $120-million libel suit against the CBS television network over a broadcast called "The Uncounted Enemy: A Vietnam Deception." The report claimed that while in Vietnam Westmoreland had duped the president, Congress, and the American people by understating the size of the enemy forces he had been facing in Vietnam. The trial ended in an out-of-court settlement.

Today Westmoreland lives quietly in South Carolina with his wife, Kitsy. When he appears in a public forum (media interview, speech, etc.) he frequently repeats his earlier assertions, that the Vietnam War was winnable, but that politicians and others contributed to a defeatist attitude that made it impossible to wage the war effectively. As he wrote in his autobiography,

> The military quite clearly did the job that the nation asked and expected of it, and I am convinced that history will reflect more favorably upon the performance of the military than upon that of the politicians and policy makers.[75]

Whether or not that is the final judgment of history remains to be seen.

Chapter 5

Richard Nixon

Just as Lyndon Johnson inherited the problem of Vietnam when he became president upon John F. Kennedy's death, so too did Richard Nixon inherit the same problem when he was elected the thirty-seventh president of the United States in November 1968. To his credit, Nixon did what neither Kennedy nor Johnson was able to do: extricate the United States from Vietnam. He did this through the use of both promises and threats and by means of both openness and secrecy. Like the man himself, Nixon's Vietnam policies were often contradictory—offering to stop a bombing campaign, and then threatening to escalate it in the next breath—but they ultimately did end a war that had cost approximately fifty-eight thousand American lives.

Early Life

Richard Milhous Nixon was born on January 9, 1913, in what at the time was the small farming town of Yorba Linda, Cali-

fornia. His father, Frank, was a frugal, argumentative man who had come to California by way of Columbus, Ohio. Hannah, his mother, was a devout Quaker who met Frank Nixon at a Valentine's Day party in 1908 and married him four months later, leaving college to do so.

In 1911 Frank planted a ten-acre grove of lemon trees to take advantage of what was then the booming market for California citrus fruit. The grove took several years to mature. When it finally did, the trees were stunted and the fruit weak, possibly because of Nixon's failure to use soil fertilizer and nutrients. With the citrus farm a failure, in 1922 the Nixon family moved to nearby Whittier, California, where Frank opened a gas station. Richard, along with his brothers Donald and Harold, worked at the gas station and then at a grocery store that their father later added onto the business.

Unlike his more fun-loving brothers, Richard was a driven, serious child with an

Despite his contradictory policies, Richard Nixon was able to pull the United States out of Vietnam.

As he matured, young Nixon showed signs of being extremely smart, scoring 143 out of a possible 160 on an intelligence test in his freshman year in high school in 1926. In addition, he excelled in public speaking and debate, undoubtedly influenced by his father's love of a good argument.

College—and Another Tragedy

After graduating high school in 1930, Nixon wanted to go to college in the East. However, money was tight and his mother had just given birth to another baby, Edward. Under the circumstances, Nixon elected to attend nearby Whittier College. At Whittier the fiercely competitive Nixon continued to participate in formal debates. In addition, he played football for Whittier.

While Nixon was attending Whittier, another tragedy struck his family in March 1933, when his brother Harold died of tuberculosis. The untimely death of yet another sibling deeply affected Nixon, as his mother later recalled: "He sank into a deep, impenetrable silence. From that time on, it seemed Richard was trying to be three sons in one, striving even harder than before to make up to his father and me for our loss."[76]

Nixon's hard work paid off, when in 1934 he graduated from Whittier second

intense desire to succeed in school. This desire was intensified in 1925, when his younger brother Arthur died of tubercular encephalitis. Richard redoubled his academic efforts, trying to assuage his parents' grief by increasing their reason to be proud of him.

in his class. Nixon had ambitions to be a lawyer, and he spent the next three years studying law at Duke University in North Carolina, where he had been given a full-tuition scholarship. However, upon graduation he discovered to his surprise that Duke's reputation was not strong enough to land him a job with the top law firms in New York City, which mostly hired graduates from Ivy League schools such as Harvard and Yale. Returning to Whittier in the summer of 1937, Nixon passed the California bar exam and joined a local law firm, where he settled down to practice estate law.

Not long after returning to Whittier, Nixon met schoolteacher Thelma Catherine ("Pat") Ryan, and in 1940, the couple married. It might have seemed to some that Nixon had found the ideal situation, yet although he had already become a full partner in his law firm, Nixon chaffed at the tedious pace of a practice in estate law. Brimming with ambition and energy, he longed to enter politics. With that goal in mind, Nixon joined civic organizations such as the Kiwanis Club and the Chamber of Commerce, trying to become better known locally and keeping an eye out for any political opportunity that presented itself.

Nixon's networking efforts soon paid off when he heard a rumor that the local representative

to the California State Assembly might not run for reelection. Immediately Nixon launched a vigorous campaign for the office, making his name and face known by driving across the district on his own time and speaking to small groups. The effort stopped when the incumbent decided to run again after all, but Nixon's drive and

Quickly growing tired of practicing estate law, Richard Nixon sought to enter the world of politics.

ambition had brought him to the attention of local Republicans.

The Race against Voorhis

In spite of his desire to hold public office, the young lawyer had to put his quest on hold for several years, while he served in the U.S. Navy during World War II. But although Nixon was gone from Whittier during those years, his hankering for elected office was remembered by the local Republicans. In September 1945, those memories opened the door for the beginning of his political career. Even before his discharge from the navy, Nixon received a letter asking if he was interested in representing California's twelfth district in Congress as a Republican. The incumbent was Democrat Jerry Voorhis, a staunch supporter of President Franklin D. Roosevelt's New Deal programs. Voorhis was highly popular, and many Republicans considered him unbeatable. "Nobody wanted to run," recalled attorney Stanley Barnes, who had previously declined the opportunity. "They asked a lot of other people to run, but they wouldn't do it."[77]

But Nixon was unfazed by the discouraging picture. "An aggressive, vigorous campaign on a platform of practical liberalism should be the antidote the people have been looking for to take the place of Voorhis's particular brand of New Deal idealism,"[78] he said.

Receiving the Republican nomination in 1946, Nixon began the campaign as a huge underdog against Voorhis. However,

Nixon turned things around by subtly linking the incumbent with communism. Desperately Voorhis tried to deny the false allegations that Nixon spread, but the voters refused to listen. With the Soviet Union slowly pulling the Iron Curtain across Eastern Europe and hysteria about communism on the rise throughout America, Nixon had fashioned a trap from which Voorhis could not escape. On Election Day, Nixon trounced the "unbeatable" incumbent, winning 57 percent of the vote.

Meteoric Rise

The election of 1946 put Republicans in control of both houses of Congress for the first time since 1928. One of their goals was to launch a full-scale war on supposed Communist influence in America. Consequently, when the time came to parcel out committee assignments, Nixon's fierce anticommunist rhetoric in the Voorhis election earned him a seat on the House Committee on Un-American Activities (HUAC), which was given the job of removing "the Red menace from America"[79] by Speaker of the House Joe Martin. HUAC held many highly publicized hearings into alleged Communist influence in government, business, labor, and entertainment, with Nixon an extremely visible presence. One of these hearings vaulted Nixon to national fame.

In 1948, HUAC accused former State Department official Alger Hiss of having Communist ties. When he denied under oath having such connections Nixon produced evidence suggesting Hiss had lied.

That evidence was of questionable value, but eventually Hiss was prosecuted and convicted of perjury for his testimony to HUAC. Some observers believed Hiss was framed, but Nixon's dogged cross-examinations of Hiss stamped him as a rising star in the Republican Party.

Nixon easily won reelection in 1948, but he knew advancement to a leadership role in the House would take years—far too slow a pace for Nixon's white-hot ambition. Therefore, in 1950 he decided to run for the U.S. Senate. His opponent was Democratic Congresswoman Helen Gahagan Douglas, a former Broadway star and one of the House's most liberal members. In the election Nixon repeated the tactics used against Voorhis, branding Douglas as "pink"—a Communist sympathizer. As one release from his campaign headquarters said: "How can Helen Douglas, capable actress that she is, take up so strange a role as a foe of communism . . . when she has so deservedly earned the title of 'the pink lady'?"[80] To drive home the point, Nixon's campaign produced an examination of Douglas's voting record printed on pink paper.

As Voorhis had done, Douglas angrily denied these charges. But also like the Voorhis case, the wave of anticommunist hysteria that was sweeping the United States overwhelmed her protests. Nixon won the election in a landslide, garnering 59 percent of the votes to Douglas's 40 percent.

Within six years, Nixon had risen from being a small-town California lawyer to a member of the U.S. Senate. But the mudslinging election victories had damaged his personal credibility. As biographer Roger Morris wrote: "Seemingly without peer in the GOP, he was also singularly disturbing, in the emerging shadow of questions about technique, integrity and character."[81]

Checkers

Nixon soon found that even though the senate had fewer members than the House, the path to true power was just as slow. Rumors flew that he was planning to run for governor of California in 1954, but in July 1952, Republican presidential nominee Dwight Eisenhower tapped Nixon to be his running mate. The choice seemed logical: Nixon was from a large and important state that the Republicans wanted to carry in the election, he had a national reputation as a foe of communism, he was a good campaigner, and he had legislative experience.

No sooner had the Eisenhower/Nixon campaign gotten under way when it was rocked by sensational allegations that a group of rich California business owners had established a secret fund for Nixon, enabling him to live a lifestyle far beyond his means. With Eisenhower campaigning on a theme of honest government and cleaning up Democratic cronyism in Washington, it seemed as if his vice-presidential candidate was in the pockets of rich supporters.

Nixon tried to dismiss the money as being meant to pay for legitimate expenses in-

Richard Nixon relaxes at home with "Checkers," a gift to his family from supporters.

curred that he did not want to bill the government for. Still, pressure quickly mounted for him to resign from the ticket because of the appearance of corruption. Eisenhower seemed to distance himself from his running mate, as his comments stopped well short of wholehearted support, saying, "Of what avail is it for us to carry on this crusade against this business of what has been going on in Washington if we, ourselves, aren't as clean as a hound's tooth?"[82]

With his political career hanging in the balance, on September 23, 1952, Nixon took his defense directly to the nation in a televised speech. He denied living lavishly, listed his financial assets and liabilities, and then told the audience that he had indeed received one gift, a little dog that his daughter had named "Checkers." "I just want to say this right now, that regardless of what they say about it, we're gonna keep it,"[83] Nixon said.

This so-called "Checkers" speech, both defiant and apologetic, unleashed a torrent of public sympathy for Nixon and Eisenhower kept him on the ticket. The Republicans won a resounding victory in November.

Decline and Comeback

For the next eight years, Nixon served as Eisenhower's vice president. Rather than return to private life at the end of his second term, in 1960 Nixon ran as the Republican Party's presidential candidate. In one of the closest elections in American history, Nixon lost to Democrat John F. Kennedy by just 112,803 popular votes.

Nixon returned to California, and unwilling to give up on politics, in 1962 ran for governor against Democrat Edmund "Pat" Brown. Nixon was badly beaten, and bitter over his loss. He blamed the news media for his defeat. In a vitriolic press conference, Nixon vowed that he was finished with politics, telling the assembled reporters: "You won't have Nixon to kick around anymore, because, gentlemen, this is my last press conference."[84] Many observers believed that his political career was indeed over.

In reality, however, this was the beginning of Nixon's political renaissance. Still a surefire draw at political fund-raisers, Nixon worked tirelessly on behalf of Republican congressional candidates in both the 1964 and 1966 elections. By 1968 these efforts had gained him the support of many party members. Nixon was also helped by the fact that many Republicans viewed him as a moderate alternative to both the conservative Ronald Reagan and the liberal Nelson Rockefeller, both of whom were vying for the presidential nomination that year.

Nixon's opponent, Vice President Hubert Humphrey, was an effective campaigner, but he was hamstrung by the unpopularity of President Lyndon Johnson and the Vietnam War, which seemed to have turned into a bloody stalemate. Nixon pledged to not only end the war but also win the peace, two ideas that greatly appealed to many Americans. A press account that he had a secret plan to end the war also aided him. In another close presidential election, American voters chose Nixon by just a half-million votes.

Mixed Messages

In reality, Nixon did not have a secret plan to end the war—the press story had been wrong, and Nixon never bothered to correct it. What he did have was a tactic that he called the Madman Theory. As he told his aide, H. R. Haldeman,

I want the North Vietnamese to believe that I've reached the point where I might do *anything* to stop the war. We'll just slip the word to them that, "for God's sake, you know Nixon is obsessed about Communism. We can't restrain him when he's angry—and he has his hand on the nuclear button," and Ho Chi Minh himself will be in Paris in two days begging for peace.[85]

Other than the Madman Theory, Nixon's policy toward Vietnam was remarkably similar to Johnson's. Although he thought a military victory was impossible, Nixon—like Johnson—did not intend to become the first American president to lose a war. This ruled out a unilateral withdrawal of U.S. forces.

As Johnson had done, Nixon tried a carrot-and-stick approach in Vietnam. He would offer to reduce U.S. bombing of North Vietnam in return for progress in peace negotiations, then threaten military escalation if progress was not made. Like Johnson, Nixon seized on the idea of making the South Vietnamese take on more and more responsibility for combat, which allowed him to start bringing U.S. troops home.

However, this policy—known as Vietnamization—presented Nixon with a paradox: It reduced the American military presence at the precise time that Nixon was trying to use the threat of that presence to prod the Communists into ending the war. Thus, even while he was withdrawing

troops, Nixon still had to prove to North Vietnam that American military might remained substantial and could be used against them at any time. The solution to this contradictory situation suited Nixon's

Nixon wanted to show North Vietnam that he would use every method (including paratroopers) at his disposal to end the war.

taste for subtlety and secrecy in conducting U.S. foreign policy.

In June 1969, Nixon announced that twenty-five thousand American combat troops would be withdrawn from Vietnam by the end of August and replaced by South Vietnamese troops under Vietnamization. This withdrawal, along with another forty thousand announced three months later, temporarily muted the domestic antiwar movement and signaled to a war-weary American public that the conflict might be winding down. What no one knew was that three months earlier, Nixon had ordered the secret bombing of North Vietnamese bases in Cambodia.

Another example of Nixon's penchant for conducting foreign policy out of the public eye while sending carrot-and-stick messages was his secret correspondence to North Vietnam in July 1969, emphasizing his desire for what he called a just peace. However, in the same message was a threat to escalate the war if peace was not forthcoming. While North Vietnam's leaders in Hanoi appeared unimpressed by the threat, they agreed to begin secret peace talks with Nixon's National Security Advisor Henry Kissinger, away from the publicity accompanying the official negotiations in Paris.

As 1969 ebbed, hopes for peace faded, and the antiwar movement in the United States began reasserting itself. On October 15, approximately 1 million Americans participated in protest rallies against the war. One month later, 250,000 antiwar activists marched in Washington, D.C. Just as Johnson had done, Nixon was forced to alter his schedule and travels to avoid protesters. The president fretted that, like Johnson, he too would become a prisoner of the antiwar movement.

The Cambodian Invasion

Even though peace in Vietnam seemed distant in early 1970, there were several positive developments: Troops were being withdrawn, the ARVN (South Vietnamese Army) was performing better in combat, and the Communists had not won any significant military victories.

Yet Nixon worried that with Vietnamization gaining momentum and public pressure forcing him to continue the troop withdrawals, he lacked the leverage to force the Communists to negotiate. Instead of bargaining for an American troop withdrawal, all they had to do was wait. Thus, Nixon needed a way to show the Communists that the United States was not abandoning South Vietnam. "As 1970 began," Nixon later wrote, "I felt that we had to think about initiatives we could undertake to show the enemy that we were still serious about our commitment in Vietnam."[86]

The action he chose was an invasion of the neutral, neighboring country of Cambodia on April 30, 1970. The operation was undertaken ostensibly to clean out North Vietnamese supply bases and to support pro-American Cambodian leader Lon Nol, who had taken power via a coup in March and whose small army was fighting Communist rebels. Nixon called it an incursion rather than an invasion, explaining that it would send a message to the North Vietnamese that "we will not be humiliated. We will not be defeated."[87]

Although the Cambodian invasion did result in short-term military gains, particularly the capture of stockpiled arms, ammunition, and supplies, it also reinvigorated the antiwar movement. In a bloody climax to a series of protests at colleges and universities across America, four students at Kent State University were killed on May 4, 1970,

Four students were killed at Kent State University during a protest of the U.S. invasion of Cambodia.

when soldiers in the National Guard assigned to control a large demonstration fired into a crowd of protesters.

The antiwar protests frustrated Nixon, who felt powerless against them. Although just a few days earlier he had dismissed student protesters as "bums blowing up campuses,"[88] on a whim in the predawn hours of May 9, he visited some antiwar activists keeping a vigil at the Lincoln Memorial. His purpose, he later said, was to try and communicate with them.

> I knew that young people today were searching, as I was searching forty years ago, for . . . the great mystery of life . . . . I didn't have the answer. . . . I just wanted to be sure that all of

them realized that ending the war, and cleaning up the streets and the air and the water, was not going to solve spiritual hunger which all of us have.[89]

Stalemate Brings a New Tactic

Although Nixon pulled American troops out of Cambodia in June, both the war and Kissinger's secret peace talks hit a stalemate. By October 1970, the president had withdrawn approximately 165,000 American troops from Vietnam, with 90,000 more to return the following spring, yet peace was no closer. Searching for another tactic, that month Nixon announced America's willingness to accept a cease-fire. In this cease-fire both sides would stop shooting and remain where they were without withdrawing while an international conference devised a peace plan.

The problem with this proposal was that such a cease-fire terrified South Vietnamese President Nguyen Van Thieu, because it allowed the Communist troops already in his country to remain there, where they would pose a constant threat to him. It also represented a shift in the long-standing demand of the United States that North Vietnamese troops withdraw from the South as a prerequisite for peace—apparently an enormous concession to the Communists. However, the next day Nixon told reporters that the standstill cease-fire was also tied to the total withdrawal of both sides' forces. The

Communists rejected the idea, and continued to insist that mutual withdrawal was not acceptable. Thieu's government, the Communist negotiators insisted, must be removed before peace could be achieved.

As the war dragged on, Nixon continued worrying about the antiwar protesters who seemed ever-present outside the White House. He felt that the only way he could keep the antiwar movement at bay and keep public opinion on his side was to continue withdrawing U.S. troops, even though by doing so he was limiting America's military options in Vietnam.

In fact, the gradual Vietnamization of the war was not going smoothly. In the spring of 1971, a mission by the ARVN into neighboring Laos to destroy stockpiles of supplies belonging to the Communists had been a near disaster for the seventeen thousand-man force, which wound up retreating in the face of stiff resistance from 40,000 Communist troops. Far from showing how well the South Vietnamese military performed, the mission revealed how poorly their troops and commanders did under fire, despite years of U.S. training. Yet Vietnamization had acquired a momentum of its own, and because of public support for the policy, Nixon had no choice but to label the Laos invasion a success and announce another round of troop cuts.

Meanwhile, Kissinger's secret peace talks dragged on throughout 1971, as did the formal negotiations in Paris. One positive development of the dramatic reduction in American troops, however, was the decline in American combat deaths that year; they dropped to 1,380, as compared to 4,221 in 1970.

But the slow pace of the peace talks frustrated the president, who was concerned about being defeated for reelection in 1972 if he did not end the war. As 1972 dawned, the prospect of defeat seemed real: Polls showed that Democratic senator Edmund Muskie, the front-runner for his party's presidential nomination, had pulled even with Nixon. Trying to restore his political advantage, on January 13, 1972, Nixon announced that another 70,000 troops would be pulled out of Vietnam by May 1, thus reducing the U.S. combat presence from 545,000 when he had taken office to 64,500. He followed this announcement on January 25 by publicly revealing Kissinger's secret peace talks. Both of these actions had the desired effect, causing him to surge four points ahead of Muskie in the polls.

An ARVN soldier patrols the Vietnamese countryside. Vietnamization consisted of the ARVN gradually taking over the responsibilities carried out by U.S. troops.

Seeking Support

Nixon had long hoped that the Soviet Union and China might influence North Vietnam to seek peace. To that end, in February 1972, Nixon made a historic trip to China. He then announced plans for another groundbreaking trip to Moscow in May to improve United States–Soviet rela-

tions. These initiatives had the opposite effect from what Nixon had hoped for. Anticipating that Nixon's visits would result in pressure from their Russian and Chinese allies to end the war, the North Vietnamese unleashed a massive spring offensive in

South Vietnam on March 30, 1972, to gain as much ground as possible. Approximately 120,000 North Vietnamese troops and thousands of Viet Cong launched a three-pronged attack that they hoped would rout the ARVN, prove the failure of Vietnamization, and illustrate to the United States that a negotiated settlement on their terms was the only way to end the war.

Because the United States had too few combat troops left to counter the Communist offensive, Nixon authorized an intensive bombing campaign against North Vietnam. He also ordered the mining of numerous North Vietnamese ports to prevent military supplies from coming into the country.

Although the ARVN sometimes fought well during this offensive, it was U.S. air power and assistance from American advisors that prevented defeat at the hands of the Communists. Nixon noted the difference between the two sides in his diary, writing: "The real problem is that the enemy is willing to sacrifice in order to win, while the South Vietnamese simply aren't willing to pay that much of a price in order to avoid losing."[90]

The Communists were willing to pay a high price indeed, losing an estimated 83,000 troops during the three-month offensive, compared to 15,000 South Vietnamese dead. Although the offensive neither shattered the South's forces nor toppled Thieu's government, it enabled the Communists to increase the share of territory that they held in South Vietnam from 3.7 percent to 9.7 percent. It also demonstrated to Thieu that once the United States completely pulled out of his country he would have a difficult time holding off the Communists, especially if a final peace treaty allowed them to retain territory they had already won in the south.

A Peace Agreement Is Reached

Realizing that they could not defeat the South Vietnamese while American air power supported them, and having gained more territory, the North Vietnamese were now ready to negotiate a settlement. Talks between Kissinger and North Vietnam's chief negotiator Le Duc Tho gained momentum. On October 8, 1972, both sides agreed on the basic framework for a treaty that included an immediate cease-fire, a unilateral withdrawal of all American troops from South Vietnam, and the return of all prisoners of war.

However, when Thieu learned that the agreement did not require North Vietnamese troops to withdraw from his country, he refused to sign it and demanded sixty-nine changes to the treaty. The North Vietnamese rejected these demands, and talks between Kissinger and Tho broke down again in early December. To force the North Vietnamese back to the bargaining table, Nixon unleashed another intensive bombing campaign on North Vietnam. In late December, the Communists agreed to more talks, and on January 23, 1973, an agreement was reached be-

North Vietnamese chief negotiator Le Duc Tho (left) and Henry Kissinger shake hands after reaching an agreement to end the Vietnam War.

tween the two sides. Despite Thieu's objections and the bombing campaign, this agreement was nearly identical to the one reached in October.

Nixon's strategy for dealing with Thieu during the last stage of negotiations varied

between coercion and persuasion. Initially he tried to force Thieu to sign the agreement, telling him that his reluctance would "have the most serious effects upon my ability to continue support for you."[91]

However, worried that the American public might see him as forcing Thieu to sign a bad agreement if his government did eventually collapse, Nixon then reversed himself and sent the South Vietnamese president several letters pledging American support for his regime. A letter he sent Thieu on November 14 was typical: "You have my absolute assurance that if Hanoi fails to abide by the terms of this agreement it is my intention to take swift and severe retaliatory action." At the end of that same letter, Nixon said, "I repeat my personal assurance to you that the United States will react very strongly and rapidly to any violation of the agreement."[92]

Thieu took these pledges at face value, not realizing that Nixon had no authority to honor them unless Congress agreed to renewed military action in South Vietnam—a dubious prospect at best. Thus, armed with these meaningless assurances, Thieu agreed to the treaty.

As called for in the agreement, the last U.S. ground forces left South Vietnam in

March 1973. Two years later, Thieu's worst fears were realized when South Vietnam fell to the Communists. Other than to provide transportation out of the country for the South Vietnamese president and a handful of high government officials, the United States could do little.

Final Days

By that time, however, Nixon was no longer president. An enormous scandal that involved abuses of his presidential power and attempts to cover up those abuses had engulfed Nixon and his administration. Known collectively as Watergate, the misdeeds that Nixon and various aides were alleged to have committed caused a congressional committee to recommend the president's impeachment. Rather than face that humiliating prospect, Nixon resigned on August 9, 1974.

Nixon spent the next years writing books, speaking to various groups and organizations, and both advising and assisting various U.S. presidents on foreign policy, particularly when it concerned Russia or China. By the time he died of a stroke on April 22, 1994, feelings against the former president had mellowed. Credited with accomplishments like the reopening

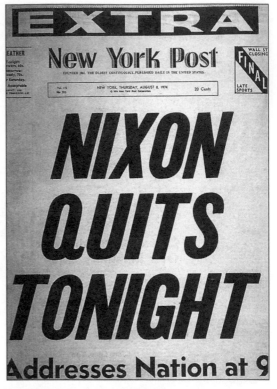

In order to avoid the humiliation of an impeachment, Nixon resigned as president.

of relations between the United States and China, Nixon eventually came to be regarded as an accomplished leader by many people, both at home and abroad.

Chapter 6

Henry Kissinger

College professor, author, politician, and playboy: Henry Kissinger was all these things and more. Yet perhaps his most important role was as the diplomat who negotiated an end to U.S involvement in Vietnam. The agreement that ended the Vietnam War garnered Kissinger the accolades of millions of Americans, as well as a share of the Nobel Peace Prize.

A Childhood of Turmoil

Heinz ("Henry") Alfred Kissinger was born on May 27, 1923, in Fürth, Germany, the first child of Jewish schoolteacher Louis Kissinger and his wife, Paula. Like his father, Henry loved books and excelled in school.

In earlier times, intelligence and a studious nature would have destined a boy like Henry to go far in Germany. Unfortunately, it was a bad time for German Jews. A tide of anti-Semitism was rising throughout the nation, encouraged by the small but growing Nazi Party. Because of his religion, therefore, young Henry was denied admittance to the *Gymnasium*, Germany's state-run high school.

Henry Kissinger, the U.S. diplomat who negotiated the treaty that ended the Vietnam War.

Through the 1920s, the Nazi Party became more and more powerful, helped in large part by the German populace's resentment of the nation's treatment after World War I and their despair over economic hard times. By July 1932, the Nazis had become the strongest political party in the country. Several months later, Adolf Hitler, leader of the Nazis, became chancellor of Germany.

With the Nazis now firmly in control of the government, things became increasingly more precarious for Jews. The Nazis attempted to eliminate Jews from the economic life of Germany; Jews were fired from civil service posts, Jewish lawyers and doctors lost their non-Jewish clients, and Jewish businesses were liquidated.

In 1935 the German government passed the Nuremberg Laws. These negated the German citizenship of Jews, forbade German Christians and Jews from marrying, and barred Jews from numerous professions, including teaching. This cost Kissinger's father his job.

A Difficult Decision

The Nuremberg Laws made Paula Kissinger realize that her children had no future in Germany. Late in 1935, she asked a cousin in New York City if Henry and his younger brother Walter could go there to live with them. Instead, the cousin invited the entire family. Although it was difficult to leave their family and friends, the Kissingers knew that the time had come to leave Germany.

On August 20, 1938, the four Kissingers left Germany for America. Their

departure came none too soon. Less than three months later, on the night of November 9, Germany exploded in an orgy of Nazi-led violence against the Jews. The riots that night resulted in so much damage to Jewish-owned property that the incident is known in history as *Kristallnacht* (Night of Broken Glass). But this was just the beginning of Nazi atrocities against the Jews; over the next seven years, the Nazis murdered 6 million of Europe's Jews. Ultimately, thirteen of Kissinger's relatives died in concentration camps or were sent to the gas chambers during the Nazi reign of terror.

Later Kissinger denied that the need to flee Germany because of his faith affected him. Others, however, claim that this experience did indeed leave its mark. According to a close friend, it made Kissinger "seek order, and it led him to hunger for acceptance, even if it meant trying to please those he considered his intellectual inferiors."[93]

Facing Nazi persecution also left Kissinger deeply suspicious of other people and with a dark, depressing view of the world. Weakness was something to avoid at all costs, he felt, so Kissinger sought out strong-willed personalities as protectors. As biographer Walter Isaacson wrote:

> Kissinger's father . . . was graced by gentleness and a heart of unquestioning kindness. But such virtues served only to make him seem weak in the face of Nazi humiliation. As Kissinger

grew older, he repeatedly attached himself to forceful, often overbearing patrons with powerful personalities [such as] Professor William "Wild Bill" Elliott at Harvard, Nelson Rockefeller, Richard Nixon.[94]

In the Army

In the United States, the Kissingers settled in the Washington Heights section of New York City. Kissinger again did well in school, getting a grade of 90 percent or better in almost every course he took.

After graduating from high school, Kissinger enrolled at New York City College. It seemed as if he would become an accountant, which was the profession his father had adopted. But early in 1943, in the midst of World War II, Kissinger was drafted into the United States Army. There he scored so high on aptitude tests that the army sent him to Lafayette College in Pennsylvania at government expense to study engineering.

However, as the Allies prepared to invade Europe, the army cancelled its college program and sent Kissinger to Louisiana in April 1944 to train as an infantryman. But once again, Kissinger's keen intellect caused the army's plans for him to change, and he was reassigned to the Intelligence Division. When he was sent to Germany, his fluent command of German helped him talk to officials in towns the Allies liberated and help set up civilian governments free of Nazis. By the time Kissinger left the army in 1947, his work in both the Intelligence

Because of his high scores on aptitude tests, the U.S. Army sent Kissinger to Lafayette College (pictured) to study engineering.

and the Counter-Intelligence Divisions in his former homeland had earned him a Bronze Star.

Harvard

Overall Kissinger spent four years in the army. Once he was discharged, he resumed his education, entering Harvard University in the autumn of 1947. Rather than engineering, however, Kissinger chose to major in government and philosophy. While at Harvard, Kissinger cultivated a friendship with William Elliott, a well-known and influential scholar in the field of government studies. Elliott was a larger-than-life figure—tall, with a booming voice and a large ego—who took an immediate liking to the studious and intelligent Kissinger.

When he joined the army, Kissinger had left a girl behind named Ann Fleischer. The relationship sputtered during his years away, but when Kissinger returned to the United States, the two resumed their relationship. On February 6, 1949, the couple was married. Ann Kissinger went to work earning the money they needed to live on while her new husband finished college.

Kissinger's friendship with Elliott paid off in 1951 when the professor put him in charge of the Harvard International Seminar. This program brought together promising young leaders from around the world who would spend the summer at Harvard listening to such distinguished guest lecturers as former First Lady Eleanor Roosevelt and American labor leader Walter Reuther. In his role as the program's director, Kissinger developed an impressive network of contacts in governments across the globe.

A Surprise Best-Seller

Although Kissinger had set his sights on becoming a college professor after graduating from Harvard, when he was offered the position of staff director of a group studying nuclear weapons and foreign policy at the Council on Foreign Relations in New York City, he accepted. Kissinger turned the work of this group into a book titled *Nuclear Weapons and Foreign Policy,* which contended that the United States could use nuclear weapons when fighting limited wars without necessarily bringing about a wider conflict.

Kissinger's book became a surprise best-seller and also stirred great interest in Washington, D.C., for it rebutted the prevailing theory that once nuclear weapons were used in a war the conflict would inevitably escalate. The book received glowing reviews and catapulted Kissinger to fame. It also allowed him to cultivate another powerful friend: Nelson Rockefeller, who was an assistant to then-President Dwight Eisenhower.

His newfound fame gained Kissinger the position of lecturer at Harvard in 1957. Two years later, he was promoted to assistant professor. Kissinger's fame also caused him to be much in demand on the social scene as well. His home was often the site of glamorous parties and dinners attended by distinguished professors, government leaders, and other notables.

But although his professional life was soaring, his personal life was headed downhill. He and Ann had two children (Elizabeth in 1959 and David two years later) but the marriage was failing. "Kissinger was a very German husband," remembered one of his friends at the time. "He tended to

In Nuclear Weapons and Foreign Policy, *Kissinger argued that the United States could use nuclear weapons in limited wars.*

treat Ann as a hausfrau [housewife], and he never paid much heed to anything she might have to say at the table."[95]

Although the two liked and respected one another, they agreed that they could not stay married. At the end of 1962, the couple separated, and then divorced in August 1964.

On the Outside Looking In

Having tasted influence with governmental leaders due to the success of *Nuclear Weapons and Foreign Policy,* Kissinger was hungry for more and set his sights on obtaining a key political appointment in the field of foreign affairs. He hoped for a job

in the administration of the newly elected John F. Kennedy, but although he published another book about foreign policy, *The Necessity for Choice,* he was not offered an appointment, much to his consternation. Instead, Kissinger became a part-time government consultant. However, this failed to bring him into the inner circles of Kennedy's administration. His biographer, Walter Issacson wrote:

From 1961 until 1968, he [Kissinger] would remain only on the fringes of power, like an outsider with his nose pressed to the glass. During those eight years, he would continue as a professor at Harvard, teaching his courses and running his summer seminar. But his heart was in Washington, as he buzzed around the periphery as an adviser to Kennedy, Lyndon Johnson, and Nelson Rockefeller.[96]

Kissinger's government work, however, allowed him to see how the United States was rapidly being drawn into the civil war in Vietnam. In 1965, at the request of American Ambassador Henry Cabot Lodge, Kissinger visited South Vietnam. The trip made him realize that the United States was sinking into the same quagmire in Vietnam that had trapped the French for so many years: supporting an inept government by fighting a war against an enemy that enjoyed wide popular support. He did not believe that a military victory was possible in Vietnam and felt that negotiations would have to take place eventually.

In fact, during mid to late 1967, Kissinger became involved in secret diplomatic efforts to arrange a halt in U.S. bombing of North Vietnam in exchange for that country's pledge to begin peace talks. Although the effort was unsuccessful, Kissinger was now part of a select circle of individuals who were kept apprised of efforts to seek peace in Vietnam.

Kissinger and Nixon

For Kissinger, knowledge now was power, or at least knowledge offered him access to those who sought power, such as Republican presidential hopeful Richard Nixon. Initially, Kissinger was wary of Nixon, believing him to be shallow and to not have a good understanding of foreign policy issues. In fact, before the 1968 Republican National Convention in Miami that nominated Nixon, Kissinger said to author and historian Theodore H. White: "Teddy, we have to stop this madman Nixon [from gaining the presidential nomination]."[97] Kissinger strongly felt that Nixon's election would be a disaster for the United States.

Despite these misgivings, however, after Nixon was nominated Kissinger reportedly supplied his campaign with insider information on the status of the Vietnam peace talks in Paris. The quality of Kissinger's information impressed Nixon. "During the last days of the campaign, when Kissinger was providing us with information about the bombing halt, I became more aware of his knowledge and his influence,"[98] Nixon later said.

National Security Advisor

This favorable impression paid off when in late November 1968, after winning the presidential election, Nixon selected Kissinger as his national security advisor. This began the political and personal relationship of what Kissinger biographer Isaacson called "The Odd Couple."

Both of them could be suspicious and secretive; they tended to think the worst of other people's motives, and they liked to pit their perceived enemies against one another. Inveterate backbiters, they forged alliances by invoking mutual enemies and brooding about shared antagonisms.[99]

Being offered the job of national security advisor was a coup for Kissinger, since Nixon had told him that he intended to run foreign policy from the White House as a way of keeping foreign policy decisions secret from the public, Congress, and even members of Nixon's own cabinet. With the president's implicit blessing, Kissinger built a strong organization at the National Security Council that channeled all foreign policy recommendations from the Pentagon, CIA, and the State Department to Nixon. Some observers, even those close to Kissinger, were concerned over the council's naked power grab. One of the members of Kissinger's group later called this "a seizure of power unprecedented in modern American foreign policy."[100]

Throughout the negotiations with North Vietnam, Kissinger conferred with Nixon often and kept him updated on the status of the peace talks.

No Quick Solution

The main foreign policy problem confronting Nixon and Kissinger was Vietnam. By early 1969, the United States had more than 536,000 troops in the Southeast Asian country, was suffering combat losses of approximately 200 per week, and was no closer to victory than when American combat troops first arrived in the country in the spring of 1965.

Initially, Kissinger felt that he could quickly negotiate a settlement to end the Vietnam War. "Give us six months," he told a group of antiwar Quakers at the beginning of the Nixon administration, "and if we haven't ended the war by then, you can come back and tear down the White House fence."[101]

According to Nixon aide H. R. Haldeman, Kissinger endorsed Nixon's Madman Theory in foreign policy, by which he led the North Vietnamese to believe that Nixon was unstable and unpredictable enough to use nuclear weapons. Kissinger felt that diplomacy worked best when backed up by the threat of force. Thus Kissinger often portrayed himself as restraining Nixon from sudden acts of irrational violence. Kissinger would allude to the fact that Nixon was about to do something drastic to North Vietnam unless they cooperated. If they did as he asked, then Kissinger could convince the president to back down.

Kissinger again made use of the Madman Theory late in 1969. This time he tried to enlist the Soviet Union to pressure Hanoi to come to a diplomatic settlement, ominously warning the Russian ambassador to the United States, Anatoly Dobrynin, that "the train has just left the station and is now headed down the track,"[102] thereby suggesting that Nixon was out of control.

Neither these threats nor secret bombing of North Vietnamese troops in neighboring Cambodia was effective, however. Just as Lyndon Johnson had done, both Nixon and Kissinger underestimated the fervent desire of the Communists to reunite Vietnam and overestimated the effectiveness of military action. Kissinger in particular believed that a third world power like North Vietnam had a military breaking point. If that breaking point could be found, he felt, then the Communists would seek peace. But North Vietnam proved to be much tougher and more resilient than Kissinger had ever imagined.

Vietnamization

With his initial plans for ending the war thwarted, Kissinger was forced to watch while Nixon sought other avenues to peace. Some members of Nixon's cabinet, chiefly Defense Secretary Melvin Laird, favored the systematic withdrawal of American troops and gradual turnover of responsibility for the war to the South Vietnamese.

To Kissinger, this so-called Vietnamization of the war was the antithesis of his belief that effective diplomacy needed the threat of military action. A strong military presence in Vietnam, he felt, was one of

America's few bargaining chips. The only way that Vietnamization would work, Kissinger said, was if North Vietnam thought it was truly making South Vietnam stronger. "If, however," he added, "we withdraw at a rate that gives Hanoi the feeling that we are really just looking for an excuse to get out, then it will thwart negotiations, because they will just sit there and wait."[103]

Nixon, however, embraced Vietnamization. Not only did it reduce U.S. troop de-

When he saw the initial plans for peace thwarted, Kissinger realized that the North Vietnamese were much tougher and resilient than he imagined.

ployment, but it was also good public relations because it showed him bringing troops home. Thereafter, Kissinger would have to negotiate with the presence of Vietnamization hanging over him.

Secret Peace Talks Begin

As was his style, Kissinger decided to initiate secret peace negotiations away from the glare of publicity that surrounded the official Paris talks. On August 4, 1969, he held his first secret meeting with North Vietnamese representatives in Paris. Unfortunately, the session accomplished nothing except for obtaining a North Vietnamese promise to meet with him again in February of the following year. At that session, the Communists were represented by one of their top officials, Le Duc Tho. For the next three years, he and Kissinger would confront each other across the negotiating table, probing for weaknesses like two boxers in a championship fight.

Partly because of the stagnation of these secret talks, U.S. and South Vietnamese troops invaded Cambodia in May 1970. Having failed to achieve results by withdrawing troops, U.S. policy now swung in the opposite direction, toward a dramatic escalation of the war. The purpose of the Cambodia invasion, which Kissinger supported, was to eliminate Communist bases in that neutral country. It was also an opportunity for Nixon and Kissinger to show North Vietnam that even though the United States was withdrawing troops, they still intended to vigorously prosecute the war.

Four members of Kissinger's staff resigned in protest over the Cambodia invasion, and Kissinger found that there was a personal price to pay as well. A group of thirteen fellow professors from Harvard confronted him in Washington to express their revulsion at the invasion. The angry meeting destroyed Kissinger's last remaining ties to the academic world.

"Power Is the Ultimate Aphrodisiac"

Fortunately for Kissinger, his tension-filled job provided an unlikely but most welcome benefit: It made him Washington's most eligible bachelor. "Power is the ultimate aphrodisiac,"[104] Kissinger had once said. Now that he was one of the most powerful men in the government, he found beautiful women irresistibly attracted to him. With his German accent, thick glasses, plain face, and serious nature, Kissinger seemed an unlikely sex symbol. Yet, he began dating some of the most desirable women in Hollywood, including actresses Jill St. John, Samantha Eggar, Shirley MacLaine, Marlo Thomas, and Candice Bergen.

"I go out with actresses because I'm not apt to marry one,"[105] Kissinger joked. He also noted that his playboy reputation helped to reassure people that he wasn't a stuffy bureaucrat.

Still Seeking Peace

Yet the war remained Kissinger's primary concern. In May 1971, Kissinger resumed his secret peace talks with the North Vietnamese, but the negotiations again bogged down. The two sides were stuck on the same issues: The United States wanted a mutual withdrawal from South Vietnam, while the North Vietnamese considered

America the aggressor and wanted a unilateral withdrawal of U.S. troops. In addition, Hanoi wanted South Vietnamese president Nguyen Van Thieu and his government removed, while the United States had no intention of abandoning him.

Meanwhile, under the policy of Vietnamization, more than 400,000 American soldiers had been withdrawn from South Vietnam, and American battle casualties had declined to fewer than ten per week. As he had feared, the slow withdrawal of U.S. troops was depriving Kissinger of negotiating leverage; to the North Viet-namese, it made more sense to simply wait for the Americans to leave on their own, rather than make concessions at the bargaining table for that to happen.

"The more automatic our withdrawal, the less useful it was as a bargaining weapon," Kissinger later wrote. "The demand for mutual withdrawal grew hollow as our unilateral withdrawal accelerated."[106]

Henry Kissinger is seen with actress Jill St. John. Because of his high profile, Kissinger soon became Washington's most eligible bachelor.

A Thaw Brings Hope

While Kissinger negotiated with the North Vietnamese, Nixon was seeking improved relations with both the People's Republic of China and the Soviet Union. Fearful that these major Communist powers might force North Vietnam into a peace agreement, on March 30, 1972, the North Vietnamese and Viet Cong began a massive spring offensive in South Vietnam. By now only about 6,000 U.S. combat troops remained in South Vietnam and the Communists made significant territorial gains. They knew that if a truce resulted from the peace talks, it would probably include a proviso "freezing" the opposing forces in place, and so they wanted to be in control of as much territory as possible. They also wanted to demonstrate that Vietnamization had not resulted in a South Vietnam army strong enough to compete with them.

Nixon reacted angrily to the new wave of attacks. He intensified the bombing of North Vietnam and decided to mine the harbors of some North Vietnamese ports, such as Haiphong. These actions worried Kissinger; he had arranged for Nixon's historic visit to the People's Republic of China a few months earlier, and was laying the groundwork for another landmark summit, this one with leaders of the Soviet Union, in a few weeks. Kissinger was concerned that America's renewed escalation of the war might destroy the improved relations he had worked so hard to build.

As it happened, the Russians were also anxious to hold the summit, so their protest over the bombing and mining was mild and the meeting went ahead as scheduled. China's reaction was similarly muted.

The North Vietnamese bitterly denounced these summit meetings. The Hanoi newspaper *Nhan Dan* castigated Russia and China for "throwing a life buoy to a drowning pirate" and for being "mired on the dark and muddy road of unprincipled compromise."[107] Yet, the North Vietnamese now knew that both Russia and China wanted better relations with the United States and might not support them as they had in the past. They also realized that with approximately 280,000 troops in South Vietnam, they could not defeat that country's 1.2-million-man army when it was backed by American air power. Furthermore, the North Vietnamese guessed that Nixon was heading for a big victory in the American presidential election in November and might be less inclined to make concessions afterward. For these reasons, Hanoi decided that the time had finally come to seek a negotiated settlement in Vietnam. On August 14, 1972, Kissinger and Tho met in another secret session. At that meeting, Tho hinted that North Vietnam would drop its requirement that Thieu be replaced, thus removing a major stumbling block to peace.

Peace at Hand

From this point on, the peace process moved quickly forward. On October 8, 1972, Tho introduced a peace proposal that was tailored to the American position

in many respects, including the critical point of not requiring that Thieu resign. Peace, as Kissinger would later say so memorably, was at hand.

> For nearly four years we had longed for this day, yet when it arrived, it was less dramatic than we had ever imagined. Peace came in the guise of the droning voice of an elderly revolutionary wrapping the end of a decade of bloodshed into legalistic ambiguity."[108]

But at a recess in the talks a few minutes later, emotions overflowed; happily

When North Vietnamese leaders realized they could not defeat a South Vietnamese army backed by U.S. air power, they quickly sought a settlement.

Kissinger and his other aides shook hands and exulted, "We have done it!"[109] When an aide pointed out to Kissinger that the North Vietnamese proposal left their troops intact in the South, thereby leaving the military situation badly unresolved, Kissinger turned on him: "You don't understand. I want to meet their terms. I want to reach an agreement. I want to end this war before the election. It can be done, and it will be done. What do you want us to do? Stay there forever?"[110]

Over the next several days, Kissinger and Tho hammered out the details of the peace treaty. But just when it seemed as if the war was finally over, a serious complication arose. The South Vietnamese government had not been part of Kissinger's secret talks and was outraged that the treaty allowed North Vietnamese soldiers to remain in their country. Instead of joy, Thieu felt only anger.

"Suddenly I realized that things were being negotiated for us behind my back and without my approval," Thieu later said. "I wanted to punch Kissinger in the mouth."[111]

The South Vietnamese demanded sixty-nine changes in the treaty. Now it was the North Vietnamese's turn to be angry. They refused to renegotiate, and talks broke down on December 13.

Breakdown and Bombing

In an effort to force the Communists back to the bargaining table, Nixon unleashed a savage bombing campaign on North Vietnam. Beginning on December 18, and continuing for the next eleven days excluding Christmas Day, American planes dropped forty thousand tons of bombs on a sixty-mile stretch of North Vietnam between Hanoi and Haiphong. More than 1,600 North Vietnamese and 93 American pilots died during this campaign.

Although he supported the bombing decision, Kissinger was uneasy about it.

The United States was, in effect, bombing North Vietnam not because that country had broken its word but because South Vietnam was unhappy with his treaty. The bombing severely damaged his reputation as a man of peace. Typical of the worldwide uproar the bombing caused was a comment by columnist Joseph Kraft: "Is he [Kissinger] just a good German lending a cover of respectability to whatever monstrous policy President Nixon is pleased to pursue?"[112]

North Vietnam returned to the bargaining table in early January. On January 9, 1973—Nixon's birthday—an agreement was reached that was virtually identical to the previous one. On January 27, the agreement was formally signed in Paris. Thieu, realizing that he could not indefinitely defy the U.S. desire to leave Vietnam and accepting promises of continued backing from the United States, dropped his objections. Finally, a war that had cost approximately fifty-eight thousand American lives was over.

For negotiating the Paris Peace Accords, Kissinger shared the 1973 Nobel Peace Prize with Le Duc Tho. In August 1973 Kissinger was appointed secretary of state by Nixon, the first foreign-born citizen to hold that office. Kissinger continued serving as secretary of state until January 1977.

As secretary of state, Kissinger specialized in "shuttle diplomacy," which featured him flying back and forth between two opposing sides to broker an agreement end-

In addition to the Paris Peace Accords, Henry Kissinger enjoyed many other diplomatic successes.

Vietnam. In January 1975, the Communists launched a large offensive in South Vietnam. By April they were bearing down on Saigon, and it was obvious that Thieu's government would fall without American intervention. Although Kissinger and President Gerald Ford asked Congress for $722 million in emergency aid for the ARVN, the legislators had no desire to become involved once again in Vietnam, and the request was denied. On April 30, 1975, Saigon fell to the North Vietnamese. It was just two years and three months since the signing of the Paris Peace Accords.

ing a conflict. In this manner, he hammered out a peace treaty between long-time enemies Israel and Egypt late in 1975 and helped negotiate an end to white minority rule in Rhodesia (now Zimbabwe). Overall, he traveled 555,901 miles and visited fifty-seven countries during his tenure in office.

Eventually, Kissinger saw the end of the tortured story of America's involvement in

When Democrat Jimmy Carter became president in 1977, Kissinger left office. He has spent the years since teaching, working as a consultant, and writing. Although Republican presidents again occupied the White House from 1980 through 1992, Kissinger was not offered a government job, despite his celebrity and the high approval rating that he enjoyed among the American public. Today, Kissinger remains a highly recognizable public figure.

☆ Notes ☆

Chapter 1: Ho Chi Minh

1. Quoted in Jean Sainteny, *Ho Chi Minh and His Vietnam*. Chicago: Cowles Book Company, Inc., 1972, p. 16.
2. Quoted in Stanley Karnow, *Vietnam*. New York: Viking Press, 1983, p. 121.
3. Quoted in David Halberstam, *Ho*. New York: Random House, 1971, p. 32.
4. Quoted in Karnow, *Vietnam*, p. 122.
5. Quoted in Halberstam, *Ho*, p. 42.
6. Quoted in Karnow, *Vietnam*, p. 123.
7. Quoted in Karnow, *Vietnam*, p. 123.
8. Quoted in Karnow, *Vietnam*, p. 126.
9. Quoted in Karnow, *Vietnam*, p. 119.
10. Quoted in Halberstam, *Ho*, p. 64.
11. Quoted in Karnow, *Vietnam*, p. 146.
12. Quoted in Halberstam, *Ho*, p. 81.
13. Quoted in Karnow, *Vietnam*, p. 147.
14. Quoted in Halberstam, *Ho*, p. 83.
15. Quoted in Halberstam, *Ho*, p. 86.
16. Quoted in Spencer C. Tucker, *Vietnam*. Lexington, KY: The University Press of Kentucky, 1999, p. 46.
17. Quoted in Halberstam, *Ho*, p. 89.
18. Quoted in Halberstam, *Ho*, p. 110.
19. Quoted in Sainteny, *Ho Chi Minh and His Vietnam*, p. 164.

Chapter 2: Ngo Dinh Diem

20. Quoted in Lloyd C. Gardner, *Pay Any Price*. Chicago: Ivan R. Dee, 1995, p. 52.
21. Quoted in Karnow, *Vietnam*, p. 215.
22. Quoted in Karnow, *Vietnam*, p. 215.
23. Quoted in Karnow, *Vietnam*, p. 216.
24. Quoted in Ellen J. Hammer, *A Death in November*. New York: E. P. Dutton, 1987, p. 46.
25. Quoted in Karnow, *Vietnam*, p. 223.
26. Quoted in Karnow, *Vietnam*, p. 224.
27. Quoted in Karnow, *Vietnam*, p. 235.
28. Quoted in Karnow, *Vietnam*, p. 235.
29. Quoted in Karnow, *Vietnam*, p. 238.
30. Quoted in Gardner, *Pay Any Price*, p. 53.
31. Quoted in Gardner, *Pay Any Price*, p. 54.
32. Quoted in Tucker, *Vietnam*, p. 99.
33. Quoted in Hammer, *A Death in November*, p. 121.
34. Quoted in Gardner, *Pay Any Price*, p. 60.
35. Quoted in Gardner, *Pay Any Price*, p. 61.
36. Quoted in Karnow, *Vietnam*, p. 280.
37. Quoted in Karnow, *Vietnam*, p. 289.
38. Quoted in Hammer, *A Death in November*, p. 283.
39. Quoted in Hammer, *A Death in November*, p. 288.
40. Quoted in Hammer, *A Death in November*, p. 301.

Chapter 3: Lyndon B. Johnson

41. Paul K. Conkin, *Big Daddy from the Ped-*

ernales. Boston: Twayne Publishers, 1986, p. 63.

42. Quoted in Gardner, *Pay Any Price,* p. 52.

43. Quoted in Gardner, *Pay Any Price,* p. 54.

44. Quoted in Karnow, *Vietnam,* p. 324.

45. Quoted in Karnow, *Vietnam,* p. 323.

46. Quoted in Tucker, *Vietnam,* p. 102.

47. Quoted in Tucker, *Vietnam,* p. 115.

48. Quoted in Gardner, *Pay Any Price,* p. 119.

49. Joseph A. Califano Jr., *The Triumph & Tragedy of Lyndon Johnson.* New York: Simon & Schuster, 1991, p. 48.

50. Quoted in Karnow, *Vietnam,* p. 458.

51. Quoted in Gardner, *Pay Any Price,* p. 273.

52. Quoted in Karnow, *Vietnam,* p. 479.

53. Conkin, *Big Daddy from the Pedernales,* p. 267.

54. Quoted in Karnow, *Vietnam,* p. 504.

55. Quoted in Karnow, *Vietnam,* p. 504.

56. Quoted in Karnow, *Vietnam,* p. 562.

57. Quoted in Gardner, *Pay Any Price,* p. 458.

58. Quoted in Califano Jr., *The Triumph & Tragedy of Lyndon Johnson,* p. 334.

Chapter 4: William Westmoreland

59. William C. Westmoreland, *A Soldier Reports.* Garden City, NY: Doubleday, 1976, p. 32.

60. Westmoreland, *A Soldier Reports,* p. 39.

61. Westmoreland, *A Soldier Reports,* p. 59.

62. Quoted in Samuel Zaffiri, *Westmoreland.* New York: William Morrow and Company, 1994, p. 112.

63. Quoted in Zaffiri, *Westmoreland,* p. 112.

64. Quoted in Zaffiri, *Westmoreland,* p. 114.

65. Westmoreland, *A Soldier Reports,* p. 105.

66. Westmoreland, *A Soldier Reports,* p. 112.

67. Westmoreland, *A Soldier Reports,* p. 118.

68. Westmoreland, *A Soldier Reports,* p. 123.

69. Westmoreland, *A Soldier Reports,* p. 139.

70. Quoted in Zaffiri, *Westmoreland,* p. 183.

71. Quoted in Zaffiri, *Westmoreland,* p. 215.

72. Quoted in Zaffiri, *Westmoreland,* p. 246.

73. Quoted in Zaffiri, *Westmoreland,* p. 299.

74. Quoted in Zaffiri, *Westmoreland,* p. 299.

75. Westmoreland, *A Soldier Reports,* p. 425.

Chapter 5: Richard Nixon

76. Quoted in Roger Morris, *Richard Milhous Nixon.* New York: Henry Holt, 1990, p. 147.

77. Quoted in Morris, *Richard Milhous Nixon,* p. 273.

78. Quoted in Morris, *Richard Milhous Nixon,* p. 271.

79. Quoted in Morris, *Richard Milhous Nixon,* p. 342.

80. Quoted in Morris, *Richard Milhous Nixon,* p. 580.

81. Quoted in Morris, *Richard Milhous Nixon,* p. 620.

82. Quoted in Morris, *Richard Milhous Nixon,* p. 789.

83. Quoted in Morris, *Richard Milhous Nixon,* p. 832.

84. Quoted in John Bartlett, *Bartlett's Familiar Quotations.* Boston: Little, Brown and Company, 1980, p. 882.

85. Quoted in Jeffrey Kimball, *Nixon's Vietnam War.* Lawrence, KS: University Press of Kansas, 1998, p. 76.

86. Quoted in Kimball, *Nixon's Vietnam War,* p. 183.
87. Quoted in Kimball, *Nixon's Vietnam War,* p. 211.
88. Quoted in Karnow, *Vietnam,* p. 611.
89. Quoted in Kimball, *Nixon's Vietnam War,* p. 218.
90. Quoted in Karnow, *Vietnam,* p. 642.
91. Quoted in Karnow, *Vietnam,* p. 650.
92. Quoted in William Bundy, *A Tangled Web.* New York: Hill and Wang, 1998, p. 360–61

Chapter 6: Henry Kissinger

93. Quoted in Walter Isaacson, *Kissinger,* New York: Simon & Schuster, 1992, p. 29.
94. Isaacson, *Kissinger,* p. 30.
95. Quoted in Isaacson, *Kissinger,* p. 102.
96. Isaacson, *Kissinger,* p. 110.
97. Quoted in Isaacson, *Kissinger,* p. 120.
98. Quoted in Kimball, *Nixon's Vietnam War,* p. 64.
99. Isaacson, *Kissinger,* p. 135.
100. Quoted in Isaacson, *Kissinger,* p. 139.
101. Quoted in Karnow, *Vietnam,* p. 587.
102. Quoted in Karnow, *Vietnam,* p. 593.
103. Quoted in Isaacson, *Kissinger,* p. 165.
104. Quoted in Isaacson, *Kissinger,* p. 236.
105. Quoted in Isaacson, *Kissinger,* p. 355.
106. Quoted in Isaacson, *Kissinger,* p. 362.
107. Quoted in Isaacson, *Kissinger,* p. 237.
108. Quoted in Isaacson, *Kissinger,* p. 448.
109. Quoted in Isaacson, *Kissinger,* p. 448.
110. Quoted in Karnow, *Vietnam,* p. 648.
111. Quoted in Isaacson, *Kissinger,* p. 453.
112. Quoted in Isaacson, *Kissinger,* p. 471.

★ For Further Reading ★

Hal Dareff, *The Story of Vietnam*. New York: Parents Magazine Press, 1966. Although more than thirty years old, this is still an excellent source of information on South Vietnamese president Diem.

David Detzer, *An Asian Tragedy*. Brookfield, CT: Millbrook Press, 1992. An account of the war and its tragic effects on both Vietnam and the United States.

John Devaney, *The Vietnam War*. New York: Franklin Watts, 1992. Basic, concise account of the conflict.

Maurice Isserman, *The Vietnam War*. New York: Facts On File, 1992. A comprehensive look at the Vietnam War.

James A. Warren, *Portrait of Tragedy*. New York: Lothrop, Lee & Shepard Books, 1990. An excellent source book that examines the reasons behind the war and its consequences.

✫ Works Consulted ✫

John Bartlett, *Bartlett's Familiar Quotations.* Boston: Little, Brown and Company, 1980. A book of famous quotes.

William Bundy, *A Tangled Web.* New York: Hill and Wang, 1998. An insider's look at foreign policy in the Nixon administration.

Joseph A. Califano Jr., *The Triumph & Tragedy of Lyndon Johnson.* New York: Simon & Schuster, 1991. An examination of the highs and lows of Johnson's presidency.

Paul K. Conkin, *Big Daddy from the Pedernales.* Boston: Twayne Publishers, 1986. A biography of Lyndon Johnson.

Lloyd C. Gardner, *Pay Any Price.* Chicago: Ivan R. Dee, 1995. A look at the Vietnam War during the Johnson presidency.

David Halberstam, *Ho.* New York: Random House, 1971. Although nearly thirty years old, this is still an excellent source of information on Ho Chi Minh.

Ellen J. Hammer, *A Death in November.* New York: E. P. Dutton, 1987. An insider's look at the many U.S. miscalculations that went into the coup against South Vietnamese President Diem in 1963.

Walter Isaacson, *Kissinger.* New York: Simon & Schuster, 1992. A complete biography of Henry Kissinger.

Stanley Karnow, *Vietnam.* New York: Viking Press, 1983. A lengthy, comprehensive study of Vietnam over several centuries.

Jeffrey Kimball, *Nixon's Vietnam War.* Lawrence, KS: University Press of Kansas, 1998. A look at how Nixon and Kissinger managed the Vietnam War.

Roger Morris, *Richard Milhous Nixon.* New York: Henry Holt, 1990. A look at Nixon's early life and career.

Jean Sainteny, *Ho Chi Minh and His Vietnam.* Chicago: Cowles Book Company, Inc., 1972. An examination of Ho Chi Minh and Vietnam from a French diplomat who was his close friend.

Spencer C. Tucker, *Vietnam.* Lexington, KY: The University Press of Kentucky, 1999. A concise yet complete look at Vietnam over the centuries.

William C. Westmoreland, *A Soldier Reports.* Garden City, NY: Doubleday, 1976. Westmoreland's life and Vietnam experiences from his point of view.

Samuel Zaffiri, *Westmoreland.* New York: William Morrow and Company, 1994. A biography of General William Westmoreland.

★ Index ★

★ Picture Credits ★

Cover photo: (Center) © Bettmann/Corbis, (Top right) Archive Photos, (Bottom right) Archive Photos, (Bottom left) Archive Photos

American Stock/Archive Photos, 91

Archive France/Archive Photos, 30

Archive Photos, 7, 9, 11, 29, 44, 48, 50, 57 (both), 70, 73, 101

© Bettmann/Corbis, 5, 23, 25, 26, 27, 33, 34, 38, 39, 52, 55, 61, 62, 64, 66, 68, 72, 74, 77, 79, 87 (top), 93, 95, 99

Blank Archives/Archive Photos, 86

© Corbis, 59

Digital Stock, 17

Express Newspapers/Archive Photos, 85

Bernard Gotfryd/Archive Photos, 87 (bottom)

Shel Hershorn, UT Austin/Archive Photos, 41, 46

© Hulton-Deutsch Collection/Corbis, 18

Lyndon Baines Johnson Library, 42

Wally McNamee/Corbis, 97

North Wind Picture Archives, 13

© Tim Page/Corbis, 83

Photo No. EX65-105:200 in the John F. Kennedy Library, 36

pixelpartners, 20

Popperfoto/Archive Photos, 10, 24

© Neil Rabinowitz/Corbis, 12

© Reuters New Media Inc./Corbis, 81

© David H. Wells/Corbis, 89

© Adam Woofitt/Corbis, 15

★ About the Author ★

Russell Roberts graduated from Rider University in Lawrenceville, New Jersey. A full-time freelance writer, he has published over two hundred articles and short stories, and nine previous nonfiction books: *Stolen: A History of Base Stealing, Down the Jersey Shore, Discover the Hidden New Jersey, All About Blue Crabs and How to Catch Them, 101 Best Businesses to Start, Ten Days to Sharper Memory, Endangered Species, Ancient Egyptian Rulers,* and *Lincoln and the Abolition of Slavery.*

He currently resides in Bordentown, New Jersey, with his family and a lazy, diabolical, impish but cute calico cat named Rusti.